SKY BURIAL

Summer of '81

SKY BURIAL

An Eyewitness Account of
China's Brutal Crackdown
in Tibet

BLAKE KERR

ISBN: 1-4664-7757-1
ISBN-13:   9781466477575

When the iron bird flies and horses run on wheels, the Tibetan people will be scattered like ants across the world and the Dharma will come to the land of the Red Man.

Padmasambhava, eighth century

Contents

Acknowledgments

I would like to thank Geri Thoma at the Elaine Markson Literary Agency for getting *Sky Burial* published, and Doug Seibold at Noble Press for his editorial expertise. I am also indebted to John Ackerly, Margaret Alice Doorty, Mitch Pacelle, Philip Turner, and Kate Skinner Kerr for their comments and guidance through different stages of the manuscript. Most of all, I would like to thank all of the Tibetans that I have met. Without their courage in the face of adversity, I would not have been able to finish this book.

The events and experiences I recount here are all true. However, the identities of many of the characters in this story, Westerners and Tibetans alike, have been altered in order to protect individuals' privacy and/or security.

Introduction

by Heinrich Harrer
Author of *Seven Years in Tibet*

IN 1991, AFTER the United States government gave permission for an additional 1,000 Tibetan refugees to settle in North America, I came to this country for a fundraising tour. In Washington, D.C., I met Dr. Blake Kerr. When I heard that he had witnessed the fall 1987 uprisings in Lhasa, I was of course interested to hear more. It was the first time I heard a first-hand report from a man who was a reliable witness to the suffering of the Tibetans, who half a century ago had been my generous hosts for seven years. I had lived with them at a time when they were a happy people in a happy country, under the leadership of the Dalai Lama, who so deservedly received the Nobel Peace Prize for 1989.

What attracted me to the author was the love and admiration we share for the Tibetans and their beautiful country. Without hesitation he gave me a number of his and John Ackerly's slides that illustrate the uprising in Lhasa and the courage of the Tibetans. I also learned for the very first time of the latest and most unbelievable cruelty of the Chinese—the sterilization of Tibet's women.

When I first read the manuscript of *Sky Burial*, I was impressed by all its many fine details; but I was also depressed to learn that life for the Tibetans is even worse than I had heard. The writer himself, a young American physician, is in every respect entitled to give us information on what is really happening in Tibet now that the Chinese occupy the country: torture, coerced abortions, and sterilization. Dr. Kerr was witness to the suffering of a people who struggle to be free.

The people of the free world have read many books and seen many pictures testifying to the destruction of 99 percent of Tibet's temples, shrines, hermitages, and monasteries, and have heard of the incredible number of Tibetans who have lost their lives. In *Sky Burial* the reader will suffer with the Tibetans, and understand how desperately they need our help in their struggle to survive.

March, 1993
Liechtenstein

Foreword

Tenzin Gyatso
The XIV Dalai Lama

IN THE FIRST days of October, 1987, I was asked by reporters from around the world about a demonstration that had occurred in Lhasa. During my thirty-four years of living in exile in northern India, I had heard of many other such protests in my native land, but not until months after they had happened. China had been very successful in keeping information from leaking out of Tiber—until October 1, 1987.

I remember meeting Dr. Blake Kerr and John Ackerly in mid-October immediately after they came out of Tiber. They were the first eyewitnesses of the Octber 1 demonstration with whom I spoke. When they told me they had seen Chinese police kill unarmed Tibetans who were peacefully calling for freedom, I was deeply saddened. But I was also encouraged that my people had maintained their nonviolent resistance, despite China's use of lethal force. On behalf of six million Tibetans, I wish to thank all of the Western tourists whose hearts, in the face of truth, went out to the Tibetan side.

Since China's army invaded Tibet in 1950, one million Tibetans—one-fifth of my people—have died. Over 6,000 monasteries have been destroyed, and with them much of Tiber's 1,200 years of history, Buddhism, and art. I believe that Tibetans are currently struggling through one of their darkest moments. Now more than ever the world needs to heed Tibet's message of nonviolence and respect for all living beings.

PART ONE

ON PILGRIMAGE

CHAPTER ONE

TAKE THE NEXT TRAIN TO TIBET

O N A BREAK from Dartmouth College in the summer of 1979, I went mountaineering in Kashmir, Northern India. It was monsoon season, the season of if's, and port-wine clouds followed me up the valleys like bleating lambs until they exploded over the mountains in a frenzy of wind and torrential rain. My guide, Gulam, made rice and vegetables in the evenings and asked about the day's climb. He also inquired about how much money I made, how much money each material possession I had cost, and how much money I had left. Every night.

"I am thinking, Sahib," Gulam said, eyeing my camera covetously.

"Please don't call me Sahib, Gulam."

"As you wish, Sahib. I am thinking that you must be very tired of getting wet like this. You will be going to your home country soon."

Gulam was right. It was too dangerous to climb alone in the rain. But the mountains were beautiful during storms: warm wind heavy with moisture breaking into translucent waves across an ice ridge; waterfalls leaping off the moonscape of sculpted snow; glaciers trembling under the rain's weight. "What does this have to do with my camera?" I asked.

"You are a rich man, Sahib. I am a poor man. So why are you not giving me your camera when you leave? A present for all that Gulam has done for you."

"I need my camera to take pictures."

"You can get another camera in your country, Sahib. A better one. I cannot get such a camera in India. You could be selling it to me."

"No thanks, Gulam."

"What is thanks? I am telling you. I am a humble servant of God. All I am asking—"

"If you are a humble servant of God, you shouldn't need material things to make you happy. I am not as fortunate. I come from the most material of worlds. I need my camera to be happy."

"Perhaps there is something else," Gulam continued. "Something that you are wanting very much. Something only Gulam can give you."

"I doubt it."

"For instance, Sahib. I am knowing that the mountains in Tibet are too high for the monsoon. Tibet is a high-altitude desert, I am telling you. It never rains in Tibet." As Gulam kept talking, I remembered reading T. Lobsang Rampa's *The Third Eye* as an adolescent. My mind still harbored vivid images of monks who meditated in caves for years and diagnosed diseases in their incipient stages long before they became manifest. As a boy I knew very little about Tibet, but I had always wanted to go there.

"Gulam is knowing a secret pass."

"How high is the pass?" I asked, trying not to sound interested.

"16,000 feet, Sahib."

"And where might this pass be?"

"Very near, Sahib. Perhaps for your camera, I could be showing this pass to you."

I kept my camera. Gulam kept to himself the location of the pass. Tibet would have to wait.

● ● ●

It took years for me to convince John Ackerly that his destiny included going to Tibet with me. While we were students at Dartmouth I first appealed to John's sense of adventure with a copy of Heinrich Harrer's *Seven Years in Tibet*, the epic journey of an Austrian mountaineer who climbed Nanga Parabat in Pakistan during World War II and was imprisoned by the British in Northern India. In what must be one of the greatest adventures of all time, Harrer escaped from prison into the Himalayas five times, spent years with nomads, and became a friend and tutor of the Dalai Lama. John loved the book, but not enough to keep him from going off to American University's law school in Washington,

D.C. After graduating he worked as a civil-rights lawyer in Jackson, Mississippi.

While I, in turn, attended medical school, I found myself longing for some sort of adventure. I relished the memory of John convincing me to withdraw from Dartmouth as a senior in order to hop freight trains across the country. We lived by our wits and ate out of dumpsters, sleeping in missions, boxcars, and by the side of the road. With this in mind, in 1985 I enticed John with a train-hopping mini-reunion from Jackson to New Orleans during a summer break from medical school. Hopping trains would be a celebration: time to exaggerate our memories of the climbs we had done together in the Andes and Yosemite National Park; time to embellish our search for the Great American Hobo; time to plan our next expedition; and time for me to convince John to join me in the Himalayas.

As we rode southwest, southern Louisiana's pine forest yielded to tidal estuary and a windswept ocean of tall grass, brown in the autumn sun. As the train screeched slowly to a halt in a mosaic of cattails, the steady hum of insects replaced the boxcars' clatter. The swamp lost its charm as a cloud of mosquitoes descended upon us. I slapped the first mosquito that buried its proboscis deep into a vein. John was sitting cross-legged in the middle of the open boxcar door. He looked relaxed, more like a *sanyassi* than a lawyer. Insects never bite John when I am around.

"We have to sell plasma, for old time's sake," John said.

The thought of a needle burrowing in my arm made me cringe. Even when we found five-dollar bonus coupons in the local paper, this would only entitle us to twelve dollars each for our blood plasma. I hated selling plasma, and had stopped doing it after getting a golfball-sized hematoma years before in San Antonio. "It's easy money," John said. "We have to do it again, just like in the old days."

"Imagine a yak-intensive pilgrimage to Himalayan cliffs higher than El Capitan," I said, trying to change the subject. "We travel light, like Harrer, moving at night and hiding during the day."

"Where have you been?" John said. "The Chinese are starting to open Tibet. But even if I did want to go to Tibet, I can't leave my practice. Not until I learn how to sue doctors."

"Then how about after I finish medical school?" I said. "That's two years before I can malpractice on you."

"I'll still have clients that depend on me two years from now. I couldn't just up and leave them."

"Of course you could. We're talking about the conditional tense. *Two* years from now. Plenty of time to ease out of your job."

"It's more than easing out of a job," John said. "I've got professional responsibilities."

During the next two years I fueled John's interest in Tibet by appealing to his literary penchant, first with a copy of Alexandra David-Neel's *My Journey to Lhasa.* In some ways her story was even more remarkable than Harrer's. As a mountaineer Harrer was used to the rigors of altitude and travel under inclement weather; David-Neel was an English society woman with no prior experience in the mountains. Nevertheless, she learned Tibetan, dyed her hair black, and traveled disguised as a Tibetan woman, with a revolver stashed under her robes. On one of her first forays into Tibet, she was caught by the authorities and expelled from the country. Like any seasoned, self-respecting traveler, she ignored the expulsion order, outwitted her captors, and proceeded with her journey.

I finally broke John down. In the summer of 1987, he agreed that we would try to climb as high as we could on the Tibetan side of Everest—*if* we acquired warm clothes, shelter, and food as we needed them. During a brief pre-flight stop in New York City, we bought condoms, had our pictures taken with a cardboard cutout of Ronald Reagan, and stopped at the Office of Tibet. A one-way flight to Hong Kong and a high-speed train brought us to Western China. From our first-class compartment we surveyed the lush patchwork of cultivated fields. We also cut the speaker wires in our compartment to avoid being assaulted by a shrill, continuous socialist reveille, courtesy of the Chinese government. Torrential rains followed us from Kunming to the Taklamakan Desert and the caves at Dunhuang. It was still raining when we reached Golmud, the end of the train line and the northeast gateway of Tibet.

If the air-conditioned, Japanese-made tourist bus we boarded next didn't become mired in the flooded plains, and *if* we didn't get killed crossing the Kun Lun or Tanggula mountains, it would take us two days to travel from Golmud to Lhasa by bus. But the seasonal monsoon had migrated north of the Central Himalayas for the first time in forty years. Daily rains turned the 12,000-foot Tibetan Plateau into a jeep-swallowing quagmire. Long lines of vehicles waited on both sides of eroded embankments and engorged rivers. Going into Tibet were buses, jeeps, and Land Rovers from the China Travel Service filled with tourists; trucks loaded with Chinese vegetables, Hami melons, and video cassettes; and People's Liberation Army trucks packed with soldiers. Coming out of Tibet were trucks hauling timber; tourist buses; and more soldiers.

Once we left the salt marshes on the Qaidam Basin to wind into the mountains, seven passengers began vomiting regularly out of the windows. They suffered from a wicked combination of altitude sickness mixed with motion sickness as the bus groaned toward a 16,000-foot pass. I was more alarmed by the foxholes I saw dug into the serpentine bank of a river, the bunkers on the high slopes, and the stone barracks surrounded by barbed wire.

Finally the clouds began to clear. Dawn broke over the mountains in great columns of light, cinnabar and orange, teasing snowcapped peaks and tongues of ice from dark silhouettes. Even through our muddy windows the mountains appeared as cathedrals of light and beckoned for us to hike past the yaks dotting the frozen hills to their serrated tops. A hanging glacier angling up toward the sun's first rays tempted us to imagine different routes to its summit. We did this continually from Golmud to Lhasa; with 6,000-meter peaks alongside the road, neither of us was able to pay attention to the other passengers' infirmities, or to our own aching muscles, cramped from being folded unnaturally into seats designed for Japanese. We had been waiting so long for this first glimpse of sun that we were caught unprepared. How can one prepare for an avalanche of light?

The clouds stole the light back from the mountains as quickly as it had come. Suddenly the bus hit a bump that launched passengers into the luggage racks over their heads. Moans and obscenities in several languages filtered up to our seats in the front of the bus. A Chinese man wearing a full-length green army coat pulled his ashen face inside his window. He looked like he might throw up again at any moment.

Patrick, a loyal British subject on a three-week holiday from teaching English in Yunnan Province, also looked ill. I gave him some aspirin and my water bottle and asked him to offer them to the Chinese man. The man did not take the aspirin, but he wanted to talk. According to Patrick, the government had offered the man work in Tibet at double the wage he could have earned in the mainland. He also could apply for government loans to start a business, and his children would be guaranteed a place in school.

"We should be hitchhiking," John said, staring out the window.

"We got out of shape riding soft-sleeper," I said, referring to China's trains.

"First class!" Patrick said, with the flair of an Elizabethan actor. "That's traveling in a style more befitting gentlemen in your professions." Patrick said the Chinese army was "brilliant" to have built the road we were on with polypropylene, which would withstand the area's temperature extremes.

"The PLA built the 'Friendship Highway' in the mid-1950s to invade Tibet," John said.

"Where did you get that misinformation?" Patrick asked.

"It's in the Tibet guidebook," John said.

"Do you believe everything you read in the guidebook?" Patrick challenged. "I've been in China for a year. The *People's Daily* has frequent articles on a number of socialist reforms and development in Tibet."

John and Patrick argued whether the *People's Daily* was a propaganda tool of the State. I grew tired of the sound of these two Westerners arguing out of ignorance and boredom, fueled as much by being cramped into the same bus for days than by anything either of them had experienced or read. I wondered if after four decades of occupation the Chinese were still "liberating" Tibet; many of the vehicles on the Friendship Highway carried soldiers.

The first bus in our convoy charged up an unpaved section of road and slid, wheels spinning, into the mud. As soon as our forward motion stopped, queasy passengers dashed off the bus to vomit, the typical beginning to a communal bathroom break. Men relieved themselves by the side of the road; women sought what shelter could be afforded behind a tuft of grass or hillock. The second bus swung wider than the first and plowed ten feet farther into the furrows from previous tracks.

After consulting with the two other drivers, our bus driver then veered even farther from the road—and deeper into the mud.

Livid passengers cursed at the Chinese drivers for getting all three buses stuck at the same time. "The *worst* drivers in the world," an Italian man shouted from the front of the bus. A Frenchman wearing thick glasses agreed: "You'd think the Chinese would have learned to drive."

"On the contrary," Patrick said, rising to the drivers' defense. "These men are masters of the sodden road. More times than not they have saved us from becoming mired in this godforsaken baskerville." When the Frenchman shouted obscenities at our driver, Patrick resorted to *ad hominem* attack: "You're blind as a bloody mole with those glasses. I'd like to see you do better."

"Fuck you and your imperialist country."

"Why don't we get out and see if we can help?" Patrick said.

Without anyone's help, the drivers quickly hooked a braided steel cable to the front of the first bus. Patrick directed fifty people to line up on either side of the cable. Another fifty people surrounded the bus. With Patrick shouting encouragement to members of the myriad nations who pushed, pulled, and kicked each bus in turn, none moved.

"Bloody hell," Patrick yelled. "We're all bloody stuck."

When all efforts to extricate any of the buses from the quagmire failed, travelers resumed their verbal assault on the drivers. Patrick continued his defense of the Chinese drivers, populace, and government. Two hours later, two young soldiers who came by in an army truck towed each bus back onto the People's Highway.

We stopped in the late afternoon at Wenquan, the world's highest town at 16,830 feet. Some of the passengers yelled "*Zou! Zou! Zou!*" (Go! Go! Go!). Wind howling through the valley gave a lonely, desolate air to the place. A dog chained to a shelter of corrugated tin barked at two Chinese children, who pelted it with rocks. The dog frothed at the mouth and lunged at the children, only to be jerked back by the chain, which seemed as if it would snap at any moment.

When a Chinese man emerged from a run-down cinderblock building and handed the driver an envelope of money, which the driver counted, he said that we had to pay fifteen yuan (three dollars) each to stay the night. "This is extortion!" Patrick said. "Hotels cost five yuan. We have daylight left. If we stay here, we will never make Lhasa tomorrow." I told Patrick that he could also die at this altitude. Patrick pleaded with the driver to continue to the next village. He became furious when the driver left the bus.

"*Zou! Zou! Zou!*" Patrick shouted. Other passengers joined in, tourists alongside Chinese immigrants, chanting, "*Zou! Zou! Zou!*" which reverberated inside the bus and drew in people from the other buses. "*Zou! Zou! Zou!*" until the sun slipped behind a hill and the temperature dropped below zero. Two Frenchmen pulled out sleeping bags inside the bus. The rest of us paid fifteen yuan each and were led into the hotel's dark rooms, where the bunk beds smelled of mildew.

Outside, near the icy chatter of the river, John and I talked about Robert Ford, the only Westerner living in eastern Tibet when the Chinese invaded. In 1949, Ford sent coded radio messages from Wenquan to monks in Lhasa. His last transmission on March 10, 1949, simply said: "The Chinese are here." Several months later, Ford was captured by the Chinese and accused of being a British spy. He spent the next five years of his life in jail.

John was a talking guidebook, and he shared with me his enthusiasm for the Yangtze River, tumbling out of the nearby glaciers to wind 3,430 miles through China, farther than any other river in the world except for those draining into the Nile and the Amazon. Tomorrow we would be in the Brahmaputra River drainage system, which emptied into the Ganges and flooded the plains from Calcutta to Bangladesh, and the Mekong River drainage system, which fanned out through Laos, Thailand, Cambodia, and Vietnam into the South China Sea.

The next morning three tall, stoic men waited by the bus. They wore long sheepskins and daggers tucked into rope belts. Red tassels braided into their hair and wrapped around their heads enabled John to identify them as Khampas, from eastern Tibet. By reputation Khampas were a hardy people who had waged the most determined armed struggle against the Chinese in the 1960s. John pointed out that Khampas continued their isolated attacks on army convoys even after 1972, when Nixon and Kissinger formally halted the CIA funding of the Tibetan resistance.

After everyone else had boarded, the driver let the Khampas sit in the last row. Altitude sickness, and being launched into the roof each time the bus hit a pothole, had proved too much for five of the Chinese immigrants, who had not gotten back on. The Khampas sang and laughed each time their heads hit the roof. This annoyed some of the other passengers, but I was in awe of these proud people. I also made sure to get off the bus every time they did, to make certain our packs did not disappear. By reputation, Khampas are also bandits.

Rock cairns with strings of faded prayer flags marked the Tanggula Shankou pass, the highest point in our trip. Two more people threw up. I heard Patrick moan as we crossed China's "official" border into the Tibetan Autonomous Region.

Each bend in the Lhasa Valley's patchwork of barley fields awaiting the harvest, each expanse of steel scree and magenta slope beneath an amphitheater of cliffs, each snowcapped mountain that tore at the indigo clouds seemed more magnificent than the last. The cramps from the two-day bus ride were forgotten as we approached the ancient city. Guidebooks appeared as passengers tried to decide which hotel they would try. As if by magic, thunder from the low-lying clouds accompanied our first glimpse of the Potala Palace rising majestically above the cinderblock buildings. Thunder rattled the bus windows and the pit of my stomach, thunder that, we learned later, turned out to be the Chinese Army using artillery to liberate the monsoon from the clouds.

CHAPTER TWO

COUNTERCLOCKWISE AROUND THE JOKHANG

C LIMBING ON TOP of the bus to reclaim our packs, I saw the Potala Palace enthroned in an amphitheater of mountains. The gold on the many-terraced roofs glistened against a sky marbled with thick cumulus clouds. My heart beat faster as I imagined exploring the palace, once the Dalai Lama's winter residence. The Potala surprised me, just as it would in the morning through the mist on the banks of the Kyichu River, above the maze of narrow, medieval streets, or in the afternoon light when seen while we were on day hikes into the mountains. The Potala was a beacon, a reminder of Tibet's grandeur before the Chinese invasion. From the top of the bus I could also see more Chinese people, with their green Mao hats, than Tibetans among the crowds in the street.

The ten-foot barred metal gate of the Kiri Hotel opened into a paved compound. An international assortment of soiled socks and underwear stretched across clotheslines on the second- and third-floor balconies. Iceland poppies and roses in bloom ringed the base of a restaurant centered in the courtyard. A stern Tibetan woman at the main desk made us pay in Foreign Exchange Currency, automatically doubling the price.

Another Tibetan woman, with ruddy cheeks and wearing tight blue jeans, ran screaming into the room holding a clear plastic bag that let out a steady stream of water. This ignited a chase into the courtyard. Exhausted travelers made caustic remarks.

"The toilet is disgusting," an American woman complained when she sat on a squeaky dormitory cot. "The quilts are filthy. Only *two* thermoses of hot water for *ten* people. I demand a double room." As the litany of hygienic atrocities perpetrated against her by the "filthy" Tibetans continued, we stowed our packs under our cots. The woman fit the stereotype that Americans are the most obnoxious travelers. I had to agree in this case. John and I went to the Jokhang Temple, a mecca for Buddhist pilgrims in the heart of the Barkhor, Lhasa's traditional Tibetan section.

There we joined the hundreds of pilgrims from all over Tibet who ritualistically circumambulate Lhasa's most revered temple. Men from Kham stood a foot taller than women from Amdo, in the northeast. Monks sitting cross-legged in maroon and yellow robes chanted scripture in low, grumbling tones, while Tibetan women accosted us with necklaces of red coral and pitted Nepalese turquoise. A bald man with fierce, inquisitive eyes and an enormous metal amulet slung around his neck stretched out, bare-chested, across stones strewn with excrement and worn smooth from centuries of such devotion.

Chinese police in khaki uniforms brushed past us. None of the pilgrims seemed to notice. Tourists sorted through the tables of red felt boots with yak leather soles, skeins of dyed wool, jade talismans, temple artifacts, cymbals, and wooden bowls for drinking butter tea. Everywhere children tugged at travelers' sleeves, asking "*Kuchi kuchi* (please, please), Dalai Lama photo?"

"You're walking the wrong way," a Western woman told us. It had already become obvious that we had been wading against the living stream of people walking clockwise around the temple. "The Chinese do it on purpose," she said. "Tourists do it out of ignorance." The woman, who introduced herself as Carolyn, wore a lavender *chuba*, the full-length Tibetan dress, pulled tight around the waist.

Now circuiting the Jokhang clockwise, we got to know each other quickly, as travelers often do. Carolyn had saved enough money teaching grade school in New York City to travel in Asia for six months. She had also grown up with a Tibetan brother; in the sixties her family had lived in India and adopted a Tibetan boy. Carolyn was staying with his family now.

"How about these?" John said, donning a pair of medieval-looking glacier goggles with bug-like insulated cups protruding from each eye.

"They're fantastic," Carolyn said.

"I'm going to get them," John said. "We'll need them in the mountains."

"Are you climbers?"

"Yes," we both said.

"We want to get as high as we can on Everest," John said.

"In sneakers," I interjected.

"Could I go with you?" Carolyn asked. John and I looked at each other, and then back at Carolyn. We were smitten. Grinning like schoolchildren, we followed Carolyn into a store where she had been bargaining daily for the past week to get a Tibetan rug.

"Sorry," John whispered and slapped me on the back. "She wants me, not you."

"*Tashi delek!*" (hello) a wrinkled old man said when he saw Carolyn. He smiled, revealing a gold-capped incisor.

"*Tashi delek!*" Carolyn replied and they resumed bargaining over a pile rug with a green dragon design. Carolyn joked with the old man, but he did not go down in price. "If only I could bargain like a Tibetan," Carolyn said, leading us back into the street.

"Are you fluent?" John asked.

"Not for someone with a Tibetan brother," Carolyn said. "You're welcome to have dinner with us tonight, but you'll have to be careful. The police watch all of the houses in the Barkhor. They don't like travelers talking to Tibetans."

"What harm can *talking* do?" John asked.

"If tourists see what's happening here," Carolyn said sarcastically, "they won't spend as much money."

Carolyn told us not to talk about things like this on the street. Instead, she started to teach us the Tibetan numbers. We repeated the numbers after her and then, armed with this new knowledge, went off to shop for dinner ingredients. Compared to the description of the market we'd read in the *Tibet Survival Guide*, printed in 1984, Lhasa's market overflowed with produce. In addition to the Tibetan staples—large burlap sacks of *tsampa* (roasted barley flour), fifty-kilo rounds of yak butter sewn into yak stomachs, and freshly butchered yak meat—the market had small mountains of fresh and dried apricots, blocks of tea, sacks of potatoes, rice, imported Hami melons, and an abundance of Chinese vegetables.

"Once you go yak, you never go back," John said to a man wearing a crumpled black felt top hat, who offered him a taste of creamy yak butter at the end of a knife. "It's sweet," John said, surprised not to be scrunching his face at the taste. This inaugurated our enjoyment of the market's sensual feast. We bought a half-kilo of yak butter, a loaf of round barley bread, oranges, a cabbage, string beans, and two Chinese vegetables we could not identify.

Carolyn stopped at a table of yak meat. Nearby, mongrels sat with their gaze fixed on the blood dripping onto the cobblestones from the pile of maroon flesh. The woman laughed at my repeating how much half a kilo of yak meat cost in Tibetan, and she laughed at John swatting flies off the meat.

"What's so funny?" I asked. The woman kept laughing.

"She says I'm lucky to have *two* good men," Carolyn said.

John saw NBC News anchor Tom Brokaw, wearing a safari shirt and mirrored glasses, walking against the flow of pilgrims circumambulating the Jokhang. "NBC is doing a six-part special on China," Carolyn said. "Maybe they'll title this episode 'Counterclockwise Around the Jokhang.'"

● ● ●

Carolyn's Tibetan brother's parents greeted us with the sort of affection Westerners reserve for long-lost relatives. Dikey, a large, barrel-shaped woman, seated us on a Tibetan pile rug covering a bench and disappeared into the kitchen to fire up the kerosene stove. Rinchen, her husband, appeared frail in comparison. He poured us cups of *chang* (barley beer), touched his own cup to his forehead, and drank the beer in one gulp, with more than a little dribbling onto his cheeks. Carolyn downed her cup. John and I followed. Thereafter Rinchen refilled our cups after each sip.

Rinchen also shared with us his enthusiasm for playing *Tok*. The object of *Tok*, it appeared, is to hopscotch all of your pieces in a clockwise direction around a leather pad and yell "*Tok!*" as loud as you can when you slam the dice cup on the pad. Rinchen hopscotched our cowrie shells, washers, and coins with amazing alacrity for a man who had drunk so much *chang*. I swiftly forgot that we had only a few words in common.

"*Tok!*" Rinchen exclaimed, and we all drank.

"Rinchen used to be rebellious," Carolyn said, "before he started drinking. I don't blame him. Two of his brothers were killed by the Chinese. One died in combat. One committed suicide in prison. Don't worry, he doesn't understand English." Carolyn raised her glass to Rinchen and took a sip. "I love them as my own family," Carolyn continued. "They don't have running water or electricity. None of the houses in the Barkhor do. The Tibetan section of town is a ghetto compared to the new apartment buildings for the Chinese immigrants."

Dikey brought in a tray heaped with five steaming plates of vegetables cooked with yak meat, then helped an uncooperative Rinchen stand and negotiate his way to the toilet on the roof. Moments later, Dikey returned with a fresh thermos of *pe cha* (butter tea). She made fun of my bloodshot eyes. Carolyn joined the laughter. A sudden, warning flash of stomach pain accompanied my first sip of butter tea.

"Do you know what the loudspeakers all around Lhasa are broadcasting day and night?" Carolyn asked. "They extol the merits of the Chinese 'liberation' of Tibet. They say that the Dalai Lama is trying to split the Motherland. The Chinese never refer to the Dalai Lama respectfully. This infuriates the Tibetans."

"*Dalai Lama, yakbudoo* (The Dalai Lama is good)," Rinchen said, slurping a full cup of *chang*.

"We could cut the speaker wires, like we did on the Chinese trains," I said.

"That's a great idea," Carolyn exclaimed. John gave me a dirty look.

Another knifing pain in my stomach made me bolt up to the roof toilet. Two filthy children on the next roof watched in wide-eyed fascination as I sprinted to the hole in the mud roof microseconds before a liquid stream initiated a new round of sphincter roulette, a game that would rile my intestines throughout Tibet. I was overwhelmed by the stench, and promptly lost the elation I had gained from having made it to the toilet in time.

Exhaling my first breath, I noticed that the children on the next roof were laughing at my plight. All of my experience traveling has not inured my stomach to the different foods I encounter on the road. I had no doubt been poisoned by some pathogenic strain of *E. coli* in the *chang*. Perhaps it was the dreaded *Entamoeba histolytica* in the water, which at this altitude could never be boiled long enough to kill the germs. It was too dark to see if I had passed any blood. Tibetan toilets, I was learning, can have a marked sobering effect.

A lone, primal howl came from the alley. The howl was joined by another, punctuated by frantic, high-pitched barking from a pack of Lhasa Apsos, Tibetan spaniels, and terriers that seemed to be fighting to the death. Dogs ruled the Barkhor at night. Alone and in packs, their individual and collective yelps ebbed and swelled in a canine chorus. The same frightening crescendos prevented us from sleeping much that night.

*   *   *

The next afternoon, John, Carolyn, and I drank cold Chinese beer in the hot sun on the Kiri restaurant's roof-garden while we listened to Patrick and Dawa argue. Dawa was a charismatic, angry young Tibetan man we'd met who had engaged us in conversation immediately. "Do you know why they won't sell tickets to Nagchu?" Dawa asked.

"I waited in the line for two bloody hours," Patrick complained. "Then the man had the audacity to tell me that I could not buy a ticket. There was an outbreak of the plague in Nagchu. The plague! Tibet is still in the middle ages."

Dawa smiled sardonically and said, "Plague is a standard lie when the Chinese don't want foreigners to see things. Like troop movements, or shipments of nuclear weapons. Did you know that Helmut Kohl is in Beijing selling West Germany's nuclear waste to China? Do you know where they want to dump it? In either the Gobi Desert or Northern Tibet."

"Where did you read that?" Patrick challenged.

"In the *New York Times* before coming here," Dawa said. "As a Tibetan, I can tell you that Tibetans don't want nuclear waste dumped anywhere in Tibet. You know what really angers me?" Dawa continued uninterrupted. "I can't be understood speaking Tibetan in Lhasa's stores. In the government supermarket today, the 'Friendship Store,' the clerk spoke to me in Chinese. 'Speak Tibetan,' I told her, 'you're in

Tibet.' She didn't understand a word I said. It's the same at the post office, the bank, even the schools! All higher education in Tibet is in Chinese."

Dawa told us that he himself had grown up in exile. This was his first trip to Tibet and he had just spent a month visiting his parents' home in Kham. Dawa had become depressed seeing how few adult men there were in eastern Tibet. Every family he met had lost someone who had died either as a result of fighting the Chinese or after a harsh imprisonment.

"If it were not for the Chinese," Patrick said. "Tibet would remain underdeveloped for centuries."

Dawa glared at Patrick. "Before the Chinese came to Tibet we had a road from Lhasa to Nepal. And a telegraph. You should know that! The British built the telegraph. Since the Chinese invaded we are *less* developed. The truckloads of Tibet's forests and minerals traveling east into China—copper, uranium, oil, lead—*that* is China's development of Tibet. Much of China's mineral wealth has recently been discovered on the Tibetan Plateau. Do you know where it's going? To China! The Chinese are developing Tibet for themselves, not for the Tibetans."

Fists clenched, Dawa leaned closer to Patrick. John tried to ease the tension by pointing out that Heinrich Harrer and Peter Aufschnaiter had helped the Tibetans build a dam and small hydroelectric plant before the Chinese invaded.

"I take this personally," Dawa said. "I'm Tibetan. There are only six million of us left. The Chinese have already killed over one million Tibetans."

"An outrageous statistic," Patrick said.

"The British Parliament accepts these statistics," Dawa said.

"This conversation needs more Chinese beer," Patrick said and stood up.

"Let's go to the Lhasa Hotel," Dawa said. "It's the only place in town you can get whiskey."

"That's the first sensible thing you've said all afternoon," Patrick replied.

• • •

We cycled almost eight miles through the rain on rented one-speed bicycles. When we arrived at the Lhasa Hotel gate, a Chinese guard stepped in front of Dawa's bicycle and held out his hand. "Stop. Tibetans not allowed."

"What do you mean?" Dawa shouted.

"Tibetans not allowed," the guard yelled. Dawa stepped closer to the guard and said that he had no right to discriminate against Tibetans. The guard yelled back, "Tibetans not allowed." Dawa was a foot taller and eighty pounds heavier than his Chinese adversary. He could have knocked the guard out with one punch. Instead, Dawa argued that it was the Chinese military that should not be allowed in Tibet. Dawa pushed the guard to his limit before he produced his passport. Seeing that Dawa was a Nepalese national, not a Tibetan, the guard stepped aside and let him pass.

Dawa led us defiantly into the Lhasa Hotel foyer and up its wide swing of stairs. Our sneakers made squashing sounds with each step and rain dripped off our unkempt garb. As soon as we sank into the pink, marshmallow-like couches next to a string quartet, Dawa began a diatribe against the hotel itself, Holiday Inn's joint venture with the Chinese government. According to Dawa, the Lhasa Hotel catered to rich tourists and businessmen investing in the Chinese occupation of Tibet. Dawa despised the rooms that had oxygen to combat acute mountain sickness at a mere 12,000 feet; the restaurants that served sterilized yak burgers; and the glitzy shops that sold stolen temple artifacts. However, Dawa also liked to smoke Marlboro cigarettes and drink Johnnie Walker Black in the hotel lounge.

"I was born in exile," Dawa said. "This is my first trip to my country and here I'm treated like a second-class citizen. The Chinese are the most racist people on earth. Not only to Tibetans. They hate all minorities. Their word for foreigner means devil."

"The United States is no stranger to racism," John told him. "I grew up in Boston. After law school, I was the first white person to work in this all-black law firm in Mississippi. I couldn't believe how blatant the local officials were. At a poll watch, I caught officials throwing out just enough of the black votes to have the white candidate win."

"The biggest problem Tibet faces now is Chinese colonization," Dawa continued. "It's a deliberate government policy that has already smothered China's other minority areas. In Manchuria, there are thirty-five times more Chinese than Manchurians. In Mongolia, it's nine to one. Right now there are one million more Chinese in Tibet than Tibetans."

"More outrageous statistics," Patrick said.

"You can't deny there are more Chinese in Lhasa than Tibetans," Carolyn said.

"That may be true of the larger cities," Patrick said. "What about the large tracts of land outside of the cities?"

"The new buildings going up?" Dawa continued. "They're all for Han immigrants. Soon there will be ten times as many Chinese as Tibetans in Tibet. I'm talking about the *real* Tibet, before the Chinese gave two-thirds of the country to Western China. What China calls 'The Tibet Autonomous Region' is a joke."

Just then Tom Brokaw entered with an entourage and sat at an adjacent couch. Dawa stood up and engaged Brokaw in candid conversation for twenty minutes. We all said amongst ourselves that we wished we had the courage to get up and talk to Tom Brokaw. No one did. What would we say to him? That he had walked the wrong way around the Jokhang?

• • •

The next evening Dawa invited Carolyn, John, and me to his relatives' house. Dawa's aunt looked 108 years old; she was actually fifty-eight. She spoke Tibetan with Carolyn and filled and refilled our cups with *chang*. Dawa engaged us in conversation with his relatives by translating questions that he initiated.

Dawa's brother Tenzin showed us a fox fur hat that Dawa had given him, and a postcard of the Dalai Lama standing by the banks of the Kyichu river with the Potala Palace in the background. John pointed out that the picture had been retouched, because the Dalai Lama had escaped Tibet as an eighteen-year-old boy in 1959 and had not returned since. Dawa retorted that the postcard represented a vision of His Holiness's return to Lhasa.

Tsering, Dawa's youngest cousin, had lines of indecision marked in his face. He had excelled in the two primary subjects taught in high school, Chinese and mathematics. Because Tibetans in the top 5 percent of their class were sent to China to continue their higher education, Tsering was to be sent to a university in mainland China. He did not want to go; he had heard that the Chinese treated the Tibetans there like savages. Tsering wanted to study Tibetan, but this was impossible after grade school.

Dawa skipped his uncle in the introductions. When I asked what his uncle did, Dawa replied dismissively, "He drinks *chang.*"

"*Chang yakbudoo,*" the bleary-eyed uncle said, and gave an impromptu lesson on making first *chang,* which we were drinking. After boiling barley and letting it cool to room temperature, he mixed in yeast and let it stand for ten days. Cold water poured over the barley stood for three more days. The clear liquid poured off was first *chang.* Second *chang* was made from a second batch of water, and was not as strong.

The homemade barley beer had a remarkable clarity and effervescence. It was making me tipsy. Seeing Carolyn having an animated conversation with Dawa's aunt made me want to learn Tibetan.

On our way out, Dawa said, "Tomorrow I'll take you to see a monk who spent twenty years in prison."

•   •   •

The next morning, Patrick looked longingly at our collection of supplies for the mountains: pleated wool pants with cotton liners that we had tailored for us on the street; wool sweaters; and bags of dried apricots, roasted barley, peanuts, Chinese hard candies, fruit rolls, Lucky chocolate bars, and 721 Bars. These last were high-energy People's Liberation Army rations. We had an assortment manufactured from 1984 to 1987. "Gentlemen," Patrick announced with his usual flair. "If you wouldn't mind the company of a domesticated old goat such as myself, I would like to accompany you as far as I can to Everest before I have to return for fall semester."

"We'd love to have you," John said.

"By the way," Patrick said. "Where are your crampons and ropes?"

"We're going to try to get as high as we can without climbing gear," John said.

"Carolyn outfitted us with our most precious items," I said. "Wool socks for John, and a silk top for me."

"What exactly is it you and Carolyn have been doing?" John said. "Details!" Patrick exclaimed, his eyes narrowing. I evaded their inquiries.

Layers are the best way to keep warm in the mountains. We had found everything we needed in Lhasa: blue nylon running pants with white stripes down the sides from the Chinese vendors on the sidewalk, and thick, cotton turtlenecks and down coats from the Friendship Store. Dawa would have disapproved of our buying anything Chinese, but at least the sleeves on the turtlenecks and coats were long enough for our arms.

"What's this?" Patrick asked when he discovered eleven cans with a picture of a pig on the label.

"The Chinese equivalent of Spam," John said. "I used to love Spam when I was a kid. Sliced thin, fried until the edges are crispy."

"I don't see any stove," Patrick said.

"We decided against bringing a stove," John said. "Or a tent, for that matter. We want to experience the mountains directly."

"What are we going to cook on?"

"A tin can," John said.

"I'm not even going to ask what type of fuel you plan on using," Patrick said, waiting for an answer.

"Yak dung," John said matter-of-factly. "It's supposed to impart a tangy flavor to the food."

• • •

Later that day, Dawa glanced over his shoulder and took an unexpected left into the main street and the anonymity of crowds. "We're being followed," he said.

"I don't see anyone," John said.

"On the sidewalk behind us," Dawa whispered. "One Tibetan. One Chinese." Dawa had warned us that we could not be seen visiting the underground monk, who spent from 1959 to 1980 in Chinese prisons. If we were caught talking with the monk, the police could send him back to prison.

An hour later, our separate circuitous routes finally brought us together in front of an easy-to-miss temple. Dawa talked to an acolyte in maroon and yellow robes who escorted us into a quiet room. A hippopotamus-like monster with bulging eyes and fangs was carved over the door jamb. I found myself feeling at ease; the closed wooden shutters kept the room dark, and a young acolyte refilled our cups of butter tea while we waited for the older monk.

The acolyte jumped to his feet when the elderly monk stepped into the room. The monk had the brown leathery skin of someone who had spent most of his life outside, but his forehead and face were remarkably free of wrinkles. He greeted each of us and motioned for Dawa to sit next to him on the bench. Dawa and the monk talked and held hands. After several minutes, Dawa translated that the monk welcomed us to the monastery. Dawa referred to the monk as "*Geshe-la*," an honorific title denoting a monk who had passed the examinations for a doctorate of theology.

Large scars were evident on the monk's chest as he leaned toward us expectantly. I pointed to the scars and he showed us a burned mark on his leg, a prominent bulge on his wrist from a poorly set bone, and scars around his ankles and wrists from being shackled.

"Because Tibetans were political prisoners," Dawa translated for us, "they were beaten regularly. No one was allowed to talk to the person next to them. The prisoners were made to carry loads of rocks and dirt from sunup to sundown, seven days a week. Of the 360 Tibetans in one prison, only six survived. At first *Geshe-la* ate anything to supplement a starvation diet of *tsampa* and water: bits of leather, worms in his feces, putrid flesh picked from a carcass. With so many people dying from consumption, he learned about edible plants from a Tibetan doctor who was also a prisoner."

Asked how he had survived the beatings and torture, the old monk said that he found a way to see the good side of his captors, who were in a difficult position. He also practiced *thumo* (heat yoga) to aid his powers of digestion. In the evenings, when the prisoners had to memorize Mao's Little Red Book, he secretly meditated to bring more heat to his stomach.

The worst part of prison was not the physical torture or seeing his friends die all around him; it was the way the Chinese tried to change how he thought. After working all day, he had to attend "struggle sessions" until midnight, seven nights a week. Political prisoners were beaten regularly during struggle sessions if they did not recite the proper creed of the Motherland: Tibet is part of China; Tibet has always been part of China; the Dalai Lama is an enemy of the Motherland. "Geshe-la says that no matter what the Chinese did to him, he never said anything bad about the Dalai Lama," Dawa told us.

John asked if monks were still in prison. Without asking the monk, Dawa stated that Lhasa had hundreds of political prisoners. This monk had been gathering a secret list of names of Tibetans serving political sentences.

"How can you tell if a prisoner is political and not a common criminal?" John asked.

"Political prisoners get prolonged sentences for crimes like gambling, or being drunk. If you come back before you leave Lhasa, Geshe-la will give you a list of prisoners' names to take to the Tibetan government in exile."

The monk unfolded his hands from his lap and talked for some time before Dawa translated that all this was in the past. These days Geshe-la was more concerned about the lack of religious freedom in Tibet. Monks had to be approved by a Chinese Committee on Religious Affairs. The committee only appointed enough monks to take care of the tourists. The Potala Palace, which had more than a thousand rooms, was assigned only thirteen monks. Money donated by pilgrims and tourists didn't go to the monks; it was deposited in an account in the Bank of China. Geshe-la received a salary of sixty yuan a month (twelve U.S. dollars). Acolytes were paid twenty yuan, barely enough to live on.

When John asked about the restorations that had taken place, Dawa said that only six of Tibet's 6,000 monasteries had been restored, for tourism purposes. The Chinese had not given this particular monastery enough money even to build a washroom. The restoration that we had witnessed was all done by Tibetan volunteers. When that was finished, the Chinese government would take full credit.

I was surprised by the lack of animosity in the monk's eyes when he said that the young monks were initiates, not monks. Under the present conditions they would never be able to prepare for the Geshe. With their duties in the fields and taking care of the tourists, the older monks were not able to teach the young monks. They felt this was the greatest crime committed against them. It took twenty years of memorization to prepare for the *Geshe*, and teaching was considered subversive. Although some of the older monks taught secretly at night, they had to be careful. Every monastery had monks who reported to the police.

There was also the problem of books. The few books that tourists saw in monasteries were decorations. The majority of Tibetan texts had been stolen or destroyed. Tibetan monasteries had always been centers of culture and learning, more closely resembling universities than cathedrals. Some monasteries had hundreds of buildings, including medical schools, libraries, painting studios, and printing presses. "Soon all the old *Geshes* will be dead," Dawa said. "There will be no one left to teach the young monks. The old knowledge will vanish. *Geshe-la* considers himself a custodian for the tourists. These are his exact words. He is a 'custodian for the tourists.'"

"There must be something positive since the Chinese officially eased up in 1980?" I asked.

Dawa looked annoyed but translated my question. The monk laughed. "Things are getting a little better," Dawa said. "Until a few years ago saying *"Tashi delek"* was punishable by death. This is why some of the older Tibetans do not respond when you greet them."

"There must be something else?"

The monk thought for a moment before answering. "There is one thing," Dawa translated. "The higher-up Chinese officials are getting nervous. They want to go back to China while they are still young enough to get another job and retire in peace."

• • •

A week later Carolyn and I went to the *Mendzekhang*, Lhasa's College of Tibetan Medicine and hospital. After being paid the equivalent of eight cents, a third-year medical student named Yoden offered to give us a tour. "I am not English speaking well," she told us, taking two stairs at a time. Carolyn said that she was not "Tibetan speaking" well either, and complimented Yoden on her English. I asked Yoden what it was like being a Tibetan medical student, hoping this would slow her down. It did not.

"We are woken at 4:00 in the morning to memorize while the mind is fresh," Yoden said. "The four root texts alone are 1,140 pages in length. At seven our instructors quiz us on what we have learned, and we have our first cup of butter tea. Then all students gather in the assembly hall for prayers." Before we had even reached the top of the stairs, I learned that Western and Tibetan medicine had at least one thing in common: long hours of study and memorization.

Yoden bowed before entering the library and asked us to remove our shoes and put on sandals. Except for a few Tibetan manuscripts—unbound stacks of printed parchment wrapped in yellow silk—the bookshelves were empty, the library bare. "Most of our medical texts were destroyed during the Cultural Revolution," Yoden said. "Others were claimed as Chinese medicine. It is ironic. Now we are getting some of our original texts back from China, but we have to translate them from Chinese back into Tibetan."

I asked how much room and board cost for one year. Yoden said this was very expensive: "One hundred U.S. dollars. The tradition in Tibetan medicine is to treat the patient for free. We only charge a fee for the price of the medicine. We have 150 students and doctors at the *Mendzekhang.* Three hundred beds. In a normal day, we see 600 to 800 patients, including clinics and house calls." I told Yoden that most Western doctors did not do house calls anymore, and asked if many Tibetans went to the Chinese hospitals.

"The Chinese divide Tibetans into six categories according to their economic and political status," Yoden explained. "The few Tibetans who have jobs with the Chinese government receive socialized medicine. Most Tibetans are poor village people. They cannot afford to pay for Western medicine at the Chinese hospitals."

As with the elderly monk we had met, Yoden's tone and demeanor bore no ill will toward the Chinese. She was merely telling us what had happened. I opened a recently published encyclopedia of Tibetan medicine to a medical *thanka* (painting) that depicted the metamorphosis of the human embryo from primordial to amphibian to mammalian form. "This medical *thanka* describes the weekly development of the fetus," Yoden explained, "including the nature of its consciousness. There are techniques for determining a child's sex before birth, medicines to accelerate labor, reduce pain, and guard against post-partum infection. But all of the writing is in Chinese. Only the captions are in Tibetan."

I asked how much the book cost. "I am afraid this book is too expensive. More than a hundred yuan." I bought one to mail home and Yoden said, "You are lucky to come from a rich country."

After putting our shoes on, Carolyn and I found an unlocked door and snuck onto the roof, where we saw a spectacular view of kites and prayer flags flying over the sea of Tibetan rooftops. My heart raced as we looked out over the Barkhor Square. At the far end, thick clouds of juniper obscured the Tibetans prostrating in front of the Jokhang. Carolyn and I held hands. Yoden's cheeks flushed crimson as she struggled with what she wanted to ask next.

"How do Western women prevent babies?" she finally got out. Carolyn mentioned the diaphragm, the birth control pill, the IUD, and the condom. She left it to me to explain how they worked. Yoden was full of questions, like, "What effect does the birth control pill have on the fetal consciousness if a baby is formed?"

* * *

At Drepung Monastery, once the world's largest cloister with 10,000 monks, the caves in the surrounding limestone cliffs bore mute witness to the handful of reconstructed buildings. Ceilingless fragments of still-standing walls crumbled into rubble. In the ruins there was beauty: a Buddha's red robes faded to pink on a piece of wall; Iceland poppies were tucked next to a foundation; a Tibetan snow finch sang from a scrub pine. Although I savored the ruins' magnificence, I could not escape the realization that the destruction of Tibet's monasteries translated into the loss of a monumental portion of Tibetan religious and medical texts, literature, philosophy, art, and history.

Confronted by so much destruction in one monastery made me feel suddenly afraid. What if Yoden had exaggerated about Tibetans receiving inferior health care compared to the Chinese immigrants? What if Dawa had lied about his relatives being killed by Chinese soldiers? What if he made up everything he had said about Tibetans not learning their own language and the lack of religious freedom? Perhaps the Tibetans had better health care now than before the Chinese came. In my zeal to see the "real" Tibet, I had believed everything Tibetans had told us during our first week in Lhasa; I was so moved that I had suspended my own healthy skepticism, and now doubts were cropping up to haunt me.

I was most uncertain about Yoden. She spoke in the calm, detached manner I associated with Western doctors discussing a patient's illness with their peers; yet I did not even know what kind of medicine she practiced. What if her gentleness were a facade for an inner cruelty? I discussed this with John while walking past piles of *mani* stones with the words *Om Mani Padmi Om* (Praise to the Jewel in the Heart of the Lotus), the mantra of Avalokiteshvara, Tibet's bodhisattva of compassion, carved into them in Tibetan script. I realized that I had become afraid of trusting my perceptions. In my heart I believed Dawa, the underground monk, and Yoden. Their stories were consistent; to imagine that they were lying was to assume a conspiracy of impossible proportions. If I could not trust my perceptions then my life, and this trip, would be meaningless.

We came upon an aged monk on a path that wound through a boulder field. A pack of dogs followed him in anticipation of being tossed some of the pre-rolled balls of *tsampa* mixed with yak butter tea tucked in his robes. He stopped often to touch a *mani* stone and pray, to finger the rosary of beads between his thumb and forefinger, to toss a *tsampa* ball to each dog he came upon, and seconds to the faithful who followed along with him. A light rain sent the monk and the dogs along a well-worn shortcut to the monastery. John explained to me that Tibetans believed dogs to be reincarnated monks who had erred in their previous lives. That explained why we saw so many of them everywhere we went in and around Lhasa.

A small boy appeared, extending an elongated metal pail into a three-foot waterfall that sluiced off a rock. "*Tashi delek!*" he greeted us. Remarkably, the boy did not ask us for a Dalai Lama picture. He pointed to a boulder with a larger-than-life-sized Avalokiteshvara painted on the rock, two other boulders with freshly painted Buddhas, and a fourth boulder lying upside down farther down the hill. "*Yakbumindoo* (bad)," the boy said and extended index fingers from clenched fists. He mimed soldiers with guns herding monks from the monastery to the boulders.

Without warning the boy shook his hands violently and yelled, "Tatatata."

John gave the boy a picture of the Dalai Lama. The boy smiled widely, touched the picture to his head, then tucked it into a dusty fold in his robe. With the aid of a tumpline, the boy shouldered the pail and disappeared quickly down the path. I was left wondering if he had been pantomiming a rendition of monks being executed, and if this boy were old enough to have seen such violence through his own eyes. I was left pondering how vividly the horrors of war are imprinted on the minds of children.

• • •

In the style befitting overland travelers who expect to be afflicted with diarrhea for the next month, we descended on the Lhasa Hotel's Sunday buffet to indulge in helpings of beef and lamb curries, vegetables sauteed with yogurt and ginger, rice pudding, and cakes. Patrick toasted Mallory and Irving, two British climbers who disappeared attempting the Tibetan side of Everest in 1924.

"Did you know that Irving had no climbing skills whatsoever?" John said. "Mallory dragged him up Everest to bugger him at 28,000 feet."

"How dare you defile one of mountaineering's greats with your prurient slander," Patrick said.

Carolyn did not go to the Lhasa Hotel with us. She had decided to stay in Lhasa until her Tibetan brother returned from Kham later that month. We had not even left and I already missed her. We had just begun drinking cinnamon tea in Moslem restaurants and taking walks together late at night.

A balding, middle-aged Frenchman with unwashed, shoulder-length hair brought a plate heaped with food to our table. "I have not eaten in four days," he said, and did not utter another word until he had licked every grain of rice from his plate. "I hiked from Ganden to Samye. After the first pass, it snowed for thirty-six hours. I had only one bread, one *saucisson*, and one chocolate. For two nights I was too wet and cold to sleep. Many times I became afraid for my life. Once I slipped on ice next to a river. I had only sneakers. I almost lost my toes to frostbite."

"Didn't you realize what you were doing?" Patrick exclaimed. "You could die going unprepared into the mountains."

John and I smiled at each other. The Frenchman continued: "I did the same hike last year. The storm was a fluke. You will not understand until you go into the mountains with just enough clothes and food to survive. It is a religious experience."

CHAPTER THREE

ON PILGRIMAGE

THE SMELL OF hashish mingled with the smell of the drenched travelers who had waited in the rain for two hours at 4:00 in the morning for the bus that would take us to Gyantse, the first city in the direction of Everest. I was crammed in the back of the bus between a blond-haired German man wearing red felt Tibetan boots with thick yak soles, and a PLA soldier in uniform. The German passed a pipe of hashish past the soldier, who did not notice, to Patrick.

"I have never tried hashish," Patrick said excitedly. "What will it do?"

"It makes the mountains come alive," the German assured him. After smoking it, Patrick stared out the window at barley fields lush with the monsoon's promise of bumper crops against barren slopes of red clay.

"There's a dragon in the clouds," Patrick said. "Do you see it?"

The German saw the dragon. I did not, more out of principle than from not really seeing it. I wanted to lose myself in the moment. Watching air condense out of flared yak nostrils was in itself completely satisfying, as were the subtle hues of vermilion shimmering on eons of sedimentary rock, and impossibly blue Lake Yamdrok Tso.

From the fifteenth to the nineteenth centuries, Gyantse exported caravans of yak and sheep wool to China and Nepal. Gyantse's pre-eminence as a trading center ended in 1904, when Younghusband led a British military expedition into Gyantse in order to force the Tibetans into a trade agreement. The damage done by Younghusband, however, was negligible compared to that done more recently by Chinese artillery. Now the fort on top of the ridge that looked out over the town lay in ruins, and only three of the Palkhor Monastery's buildings had been reconstructed. When the bus driver would go no farther than the Chinese hotel on the outskirts of town, we trudged through sneaker-stealing mud past a military compound of one-story barracks surrounded by barbed wire.

"If you want to know the truth about Younghusband," Patrick said, "he was sent here to see if the Russians had invaded."

"Bullshit," I said, and prepared for battle. "The Brits just used the Russian threat as an excuse to have wool socks made for their navy."

"I read Younghusband's account of the expedition," John said. "After killing over 600 Tibetans, the British gave medical assistance to the wounded. This dumbfounded the monks. The Tibetan generals wanted to surrender but the local monks wouldn't let them! They ordered the generals to fight. The monks got creamed."

"What does that tell you about the peace-loving Tibetans?" Patrick asked. "They were ruthless."

"More ruthless than Younghusband?" John asked. "Younghusband recorded the deaths of eighty coolies in the fighting under the heading 'animal casualties.'"

"*Kuchi kuchi*, Dalai Lama photo," we heard from a swarm of barefoot urchins, who tugged on our shirt-tails with hands covered with layers of filth and excrescence. "*Kuchi kuchi*, Dalai Lama photo," we heard, as we squished through mud furrowed by wagon wheels. "*Kuchi kuchi*," as men whose clothes blended with the mud stared at us. "*Kuchi kuchi*," beginning to annoy me as I watched a woman pick nits from another woman's head. I felt like an astronaut in the midst of a Tibetan western.

An audible rumbling preceded the sight of Patrick dropping his spotless red Karrimor pack in the mud and running into an alley to drop his pants. Cheers heralded Patrick's return. Blushing and bowlegged and clutching his stomach, Patrick said, "I'm bloody melting. Doc, what do you have for the shits?" I suggested that Patrick stick to a diet of boiled rice, yogurt, and black tea, and abstain from beer for a few days. "What kind of medicine is that?" Patrick replied, resuming a brisk pace. "I'll just have to bloody well melt, then."

* * *

That evening John climbed up a rock shoulder to the base of the fort. Climbing, he reasoned, would be safer than encountering the dogs on the streets at night. Patrick and I tried to follow. "I'm going back for a torch," Patrick said below me.

"You'll be killed by the dogs," I said.

"The hell with the dogs," Patrick said. "I'm going—" A sudden visceral growl behind Patrick made both of us scream, and I heard John laughing above us. "You're a real comic," Patrick said. "I almost soiled myself."

"Hurry up," John said. "There's a pack of mongrels behind you."

"Like hell there is," Patrick said, flicking his lighter, only to illuminate six pairs of eyes staring back at him. Patrick yelled and scampered up the slab until he reached the base of the fort, where he could sit on the tourist path. Patrick eyed John suspiciously and inspected the fifteen-foot-high stone wall rising above them. Without any jokes about rotten mortar or landing if he fell, John made three swift moves up the wall and disappeared over the top.

"Come back!" Patrick yelled. No answer came from the other side of the wall. I was scared too, not for John, but for myself. John had already done the crux; I had to follow. "You're both crazy," Patrick yelled, as I tried to grab a handhold and pulled a loose piece of slate from the wall.

"Rock," I yelled down. Luckily, none of my other handholds broke off. I made it over the top and saw John up ahead, climbing a moonlit ribbon of quartz to the shadowy fortress. When I caught up with him, I was glad to see that he was out of breath, too. "We're crazy," I said.

"Better for it," John said.

As is always the case, downclimbing triggered more adrenaline than our climb up. When we made it back to Patrick, he was ecstatic to see us alive, and later bought us several rounds of beers to celebrate our safe return at the Tibetan hotel.

We returned the next afternoon to explore the devastated fort's stooped hallways and courtyards, discovering that many of its carved wooden beams and frescoes were still in excellent condition. The top of the hill offered a depressing view of the Palkhor Monastery. An outer wall and three reconstructed buildings were all that remained. The famous "temple of a thousand images" had been blown into smithereens.

On the way down the hill, a small window let us enter a locked room of the fort containing five well-preserved Tantric *mandalas*. We studied these ancient symbols of the universe for hours. Each had two central figures depicted in graphic sexual union, ensheathed in layers of eternal flames.

* * *

At 6:00 the next morning we returned to the Palkhor. Three generations of monks chanted sutras in the central court, which was festooned with numerous *thankas*. I felt myself immersing in the experience. The rumbling of the baritones resonated deep inside my skull. The rise and fall of the young tenors lapped like waves on the shores of my subconscious. I felt weightless among the multicolored silk banners, and gradually began to feel my mind's eye rise above the floor. This phenomenon had happened to me many times as a child lying in bed. It had always seemed frightening at first, seeing the room get smaller and fearing to venture out too far in case I could not return.

Suddenly I was transported back to my first trip to India in 1979. Determined to come to terms with my strict Catholic upbringing, I had gone alone into the mountains with the Bible, the Koran, the *Bhagavad Gita*, the *Upanishads*, Lao Tzu, and the *I Ching*. As fortune would have it, I came upon an elderly, bearded man on a pilgrimage to Amarnath Cave. The man wore only sandals and a sheet. He carried a three-pronged staff of Shiva and blessed pilgrims who put coins into his hand. I accompanied him across a fleeting glacier, long enough to see him drop the coins for others to find. We could not communicate with words, but we picked wild flowers before approaching the cave. Reading the religious texts and meeting this pilgrim helped me see that the world's great religions all share core doctrines of love, and fascinations with ritual.

A group of tourists walked counterclockwise around the inside of the monastery. They talked loudly and took pictures of the fearful deities on the wall, the vulture hanging upside down from the roof, the monks slurping their butter tea and blowing their noses in their sleeves. The monks did not seem to mind when the tourists pointed at them. But when a German man came in and began doing prostrations next to the initiates, I felt self-conscious and left.

•   •   •

In the infinite wisdom of the China Travel Service, our getting off the bus at Gyantse meant that we could not get back on the same bus at a later date. Patrick asked Chinese truck drivers for a ride to Shigatse when they stopped at one of the town's matchbox restaurants. After two hours of rejections, and no luck trying to hitchhike, John sat down to read Gu Hua's *A Small Town Called Hibiscus*. Finally, a Tibetan driver skidded to a halt next to us. "Shigatse?" John asked. The driver nodded and said, "*Gomo nga*" (ten yuan, two U.S. dollars). We paid the driver ten yuan each, and the dozen other Tibetans in the back of the open truck helped pull us and our packs aboard. Turquoise nuggets and over-sized red coral beads dangled from the men's earlobes.

"I'm not paying in advance," a British man who'd appeared beside us said, and looked to me for support. "What if he doesn't take us to Shigatse? What if his truck breaks down?" The driver started the engine. When the Brit saw that the truck was leaving without him, he threw a ten yuan note into the cab and climbed in the back with us and the grinning Tibetans. Patrick opened a bottle of Chinese brandy and yelled in pure *satori*, and all of the Tibetans cheered when he passed the bottle.

Knowing that there were no military checkpoints between Gyantse and Shigatse gave us the same surge of freedom I associated with hopping a freight train. The landscape and the altitude and the brandy were intoxicating. Great curtains of light swept across the harvested fields. The Tibetans sang. The obnoxious Brit turned out to be a medical student, and he shared his flat bread with us. With a second bottle of brandy came more singing and political discussions about who was more of an imperialist, Ronald Reagan or Margaret Thatcher.

•   •   •

In 1447, the Fifth Dalai Lama is credited with having built Shigatse's Tashilhunpo Monastery, the historical seat of the Panchen Lama, Tibetan Buddhism's second highest lama under the Dalai Lama. The last Panchen Lama spent ten years in Chinese prisons during the Cultural Revolution before he was forced to reside in Beijing. Foreigners often accused the Panchen Lama of being a puppet of the Chinese. Although the Chinese wrote and announced his public declarations, which counseled Tibetans to denounce the Dalai Lama and accept the Motherland, the Panchen Lama also managed to give many pro-independence statements. His most recent and most vociferous appeal for Tibetan independence came two weeks before he died in January of 1989 on a visit to the Tashilhunpo Monastery. The Chinese press said that the Panchen Lama had died of a heart attack. To verify this the government sent a plane-load of cardiologists from Beijing to Shigatse. It struck me as excessive to send so many cardiologists to examine the Panchen Lama after his death.

Tucked into the monastery's complex of narrow alleys and prayer halls were marvelous gilded roofs, monks engaged in debate, a printing press, and enormous copper cauldrons of butter tea stirred with six-foot ladles. One might even glimpse monks blowing on conch shells or long brass trumpets. From all outward appearances, the Chinese had lavished money on the Tashilhunpo's reconstruction. The crescent moon and sun, ancient symbols of universal consciousness, still topped each *stupa* (shrine). Banners of colored silk and fantastic *thankas* adorned the main halls. Tibetan pilgrims offered *tsampa*, money, and strands of hair beneath a picture of the Dalai Lama, and spooned yak butter from greasy skins into the monastery's butter lamps.

But the golden corners of the roofs turned up in the Chinese style, instead of the traditional rectangular Tibetan lines. The printed books were censored. The bulk of the monks' duties lay in the fields, and tourists were ushered in and out of the monastery with rude efficiency.

• • •

Patrick organized a farewell party in his own honor at the Tibetan hotel in Shigatse. He had extended his sightseeing as far as he could if he was still to make it back to Yunnan for the start of his second year teaching "the Queen's English" to Chinese university students. The party made for a fitting end and beginning. On the first cloudless night we had seen in three weeks of rain, we played Chinese checkers and drank warm beer and brandy. This made Patrick long to continue with us into the mountains. "You bloody wankers better write," Patrick said. "I've never had as much fun as hitchhiking in the back of that truck."

"Come to Sakya Monastery with us," John said. "Sakya is the seat of the Red Hats. The monks there were allowed to marry and drink alcohol. We'll become monks!"

John and Patrick argued for the last time. They started somewhere in the thirteenth century with Kublai Khan's Mongolian empire. Patrick said the Han Chinese were listed as the lowest racial hierarchy, following Mongols, Turks, and Manchus. John said that Kublai Khan had adopted Tibetan Buddhism as Mongolia's state religion, and that therefore the Tibetans conquered the Mongolians, not the other way around.

"I don't know about religion," Patrick said, "but I have a lot of respect for the Chinese after living in Yunnan. The Chinese are a wonderful people."

I would miss Patrick's unfailing respect for everything Chinese. He provided a worthwhile counter-balance to our pro-Tibetan sentiments. In the West we are raised to believe that the solution to two opposing views usually lies somewhere in the middle. However, in the case of Tibet, we were beginning to believe the truth was closer to the Tibetan view. John and Patrick continued playing checkers under the stars while I began to nod off. Before I fell asleep, I heard Patrick argue that China's development of Tibet would eventually benefit the Tibetans: "It's the trickle-down theory. You should know about that with Ronald Reagan as your president."

* * *

According to travelers we met who had been trying to hitchhike out of Shigatse for a week, a pilgrim truck was to leave for Sakya from the Tibetan truck stop across from the Tashilhunpo's main gate at 6:30 the next morning. We walked quickly down the wide, dark boulevard through the sprawl of three-story cinderblock buildings that housed Shigatse's predominantly Chinese population. Mongrels charging us from the shadows made it difficult to appreciate the outline of a dilapidated fort on the ridge against the backdrop of pre-dawn stars. Their barking continued as we sat down next to a metal gate where pilgrims

were sleeping. The Tibetans gathered up their bedrolls moments before
a truck with no lights came barreling out of the gate. We ran with the
pilgrims and helped women throw their bedrolls and children into the
back of the truck. They in turn pulled us up.

Traveling with Buddhist pilgrims at last! Each time the truck hit a
bump we were thrown into the air and landed hard on burlap sacks of
barley. There were twenty-eight pilgrims, including seven women and
five babies. It took me a long time to notice that there was a young
British couple among them, wearing sheepskin coats turned inside out.
They almost looked Tibetan with their dark tans and the turquoise
nuggets that hung from their ear lobes. They did not say a word to us,
but they shared their large plastic bags of *tsampa* and pretended to sing
Tibetan folk songs with the pilgrims. Everything became an excuse to
laugh: the idea of these Westerners trying to sing Tibetan folk songs,
and landing on top of someone else with each new bump. How strange
John's and my pleated wool pants and down parkas looked next to the
sheepskins. I noticed that the same shades of orange and dun that colored the horizon were settling on us. We were being baptized by
Tibetan dirt.

"Fuck you," the British woman said, when one of the pilgrims
pinched her.

*   *   *

Vertical red and white stripes distinguished Sakya Monastery's blue
fortress walls from the contiguous sprawl of Quonset huts. We headed
for the houses across the river, where Tibetan work crews secured stone
walls with wire mesh to prevent the river from claiming any more of the
homes being built for newly arrived Chinese settlers. Painted blue and
striped like the monastery, the new houses had sticks piled on their
rooftops for fuel. They stood in stark contrast to the barracks-like housing for the workers.

Across a flimsy bridge that spanned the torrent, a Tibetan boy wearing Western clothes and a Mao hat followed us into an alley. We
jumped puddles of urine from unattended cows, saw a dog lying stiff-
legged with rigor mortis, and passed yak-dung patties molded like large
peanut butter cookies on the adobe walls. Other children, wearing rags,

paid no attention to us; they were too busy carrying the largest rocks they could muster to divert runoff around their homes.

The recent monsoon had done little damage to the Tibetan neighborhood compared to the adjacent monastery, which had been razed by Chinese artillery. Demolished houses and fragmented walls blended with other ruins that predated Sakya Monastery by several centuries. A single *stupa* remained among the rubble.

The boy produced a note pad from his back pocket that contained sentences written in Tibetan, Mandarin, and English. He pronounced each word carefully, and badly: "My name is Tenzin. How are you? I am well." We exchanged the Tibetan for English names of things we could point to, like "*ta*" (teeth), "*ka*" (mouth), "*mic*" (eyes). Tenzin led us to his house, where his mother welcomed us into a smoky room. Tenzin had a younger brother and sister, two and four years old, who sat in our laps and pulled at the hair on our arms while Tenzin passed us reed baskets of *tsampa, chorro* (a small, bittersweet curd), dried peas, and cubes of dried yak cheese. "*Pe cha, yakbudoo!*" (butter tea is good), we said, as the mother churned the golden liquid and insisted that we fill our pockets with peas and barley and help ourselves to handfuls of "*Chorro, yakbudoo!*" We delighted the mother with our appetites, and by drinking many cups of *pe cha.*

At my inquiring if the *chorro* were from a *ya* (yak) or a *dzo* (yak-cow cross), the mother ordered Tenzin out of the room. He returned leading a small cow on a rope. The mother shrieked with laughter. Next, she had Tenzin fetch a bag of vintage *tsampa*, which we mixed with butter tea into balls. When we were sated, Tenzin played a four-string guitar, danced, and sang folk songs. Tenzin's lilting tenor accompanied a familiar cement feeling in my stomach. Too many "*chorro, yakbudoo,*" "*pe cha, yakbudoo,*" and "*ya ma, yakbudoo. To che che,*" (yak butter is good, thank you). I became acutely aware of the blackened fingers with which Tenzin's mother had expertly kneaded the yak butter into *tsampa* balls for us to eat.

* * *

The next afternoon, six Japanese tourist buses stopped at Sakya Monastery for two hours. Since none of the buses were full, I assumed that one would be willing take us a half-day drive to Tingri, from which we would hike to Everest. Each driver leaned on his horn while anxious stragglers pushed through the swarm of "*Kuchi kuchi*" kids. I waded into the tugging chorus and asked a German woman if we could pay for two seats to Tingri. "We can do whatever we want," the woman said. "We chartered this bus ourselves. But we are having a problem with the driver." As if on cue, people at the front of the bus screamed at the Chinese driver in French and Italian. The driver stared out the windshield. The woman looked at us apologetically. "I am sorry. There is nothing I can do."

Sakya was an afternoon stop on their way from Lhasa to the Nepalese border. Once foreigners chartered their own bus, they became possessive. I walked to the driver's window and constructed a formal greeting from sentence fragments I had learned from Patrick: "Hello. I am a Western doctor. We are going to Everest! Thank you."

"*Mei yuo,*" (don't have) the driver said, still leaning on the horn. If we had learned anything on this trip, it was never take the first *mei yuo* for granted. But the bus left us behind, even though there were enough empty seats to take us. I cursed the buses for abandoning us to another night among the bedbugs at the Tibetan hotel. We were stranded in Sakya, where the only Chinese restaurant in town specialized in greasy stir-fry soup. I was ready to leave behind its dirt alleys and puddles and urchins.

I almost missed Sakya's charm completely. The next day, when no tourist buses arrived to refuse us, we hiked up the nearest mountain. Each new rise looked like the summit, and it took us longer to get there than we expected. Finally, we rested on a small outcrop of red shale that clung to the steep scree. Sakya's town and monastery looked miniature next to the river.

A *CRACK* resounded through the hills. Another *CRACK* and sheep scattered across a steep ravine. We saw two moving forms that turned out to be children. If they fell they would die. *CRACK* and we watched the children move with amazing quickness across a slope. Wide-brim felt hats and beige cloaks gave them an appearance of supernatural grace. *CRACK* resounded through the mountains, and finally I noticed the slings the children were using to throw rocks with deadly accuracy.

We worried at first that the boys were caught in an avalanche. Then, realizing that all the noise was an acoustical illusion created by the echoing sound of the slings, we relaxed. When the boys showed us how to use their slings, it no longer mattered if we left Sakya that night or next week. The children showed us how you put stones the size of walnuts in the widened section of the black and white sling, and then swung it over your head like a giant propeller. Once it started whirring, you released one end and the rock shot out in the intended direction with a thunderous *CRACK*. Our stones flew out erratically and made the boys take cover. The boys themselves were experts; they could hit a sheep on the run from fifty yards. When they tired of teaching us how to throw rocks, they ran after the sheep they were tending.

We ran down the scree in giant, moon-walking bounds. At lunch, we added canned mackerel and ramen noodles to our stir-fry soup, and talked about the legal aspects of mountaineering in off-limits areas with a heterogenous group of Europeans we came upon, who had liked Sakya so much that they had stayed an extra day. They offered to give us a ride.

A mud shower sprayed us as we walked to the bus the next morning. Three Tibetans peered down on us from above the half wall on a three-story roof. Seeing them prompted me to pick up a Tootsie-Roll-sized donkey turd and throw it back at them as hard as I could. The turd almost hit one of the men's heads, and we were engaged in battle. The men threw mud at us. John and I whipped turds back at them.

"*Kuchi kuchi. Dalai Lama photo*," I said to a girl clutching a Dalai Lama postcard in her hands. The girl screamed. I tugged on the postcard and repeated my request. Uneasy laughter spread among the younger children, who had toilet-training splits in the back of their pants. "*Kuchi kuchi*," I said grabbing the smallest boy's belly with my enormous white hand. The children shrieked with laughter. When we had arrived at Sakya I had cursed these urchins. Now they were my *kuchi kuchi* kids.

* * *

At Xegar, six French trekkers waiting by the side of the road pushed onto our bus and demanded that we take them to Tingri. They had just hiked from Everest and had to return to Tingri for their equipment. The group's arrogant tone incurred the collective wrath of the chartered passengers. The trekkers argued until the passengers let them stay—if together they paid 108 yuan to travel the next twenty-six kilometers.

"Cons! For that price we could go to Lhasa."

"Then go to Lhasa!"

"This is preposterous."

The driver settled the argument by charging each trekker five yuan, a fair price. We were moving again. A tall, unshaven man with water dripping off his stringy, unwashed hair sat down next to me. "Two weeks we are trekking to Everest and the whole time rain," the man said. "We ,come 12,000 miles for a glimpse of this mountain. We wait in Base Camp three extra days, and still only monsoon. Not seeing Everest is the biggest disappointment of my life!" I tell the man we are headed toward Everest and he says, "You will never see Everest."

* * *

Wisps of smoke traced magical lines from the prayer flags on Tingri's rooftops to the heavy clouds that sealed the valley. As we walked to the Tibetan hotel, a flock of urchins pressed fistfuls of *tsampa* into our hands, ran metal hoops in circles around us, and splashed each other in the hotel's flooded central courtyard. The magic faded when we realized that there would be no effective boundary between the monsoon and our room. The straw mats were the dirtiest I had yet seen in Tibet, and smelled of mildew. A sordid history unfolded as I examined the soiled sheet: the first corner had been used as a dish towel for spaghetti sauce; the second to wipe blackened soot from a pot; cigarette burns marked the third corner; crusted snot clung to the fourth.

"Don't touch that mattress!" shouted another Frenchman, with a half-smoked Gauloise protruding from his scraggly beard. "*Les puces de lits.* Bedbugs. They attacked me last night." Seeing the Frenchman scratching made me scratch. "This is a godforsaken place. I am going to Everest. Today I wait all day for a stupid yak man. We made an agreement yesterday. I paid him and he never came back. They are thieves, these yak men."

We went in search of a yak man and found five of them drinking *chang* in the hotel's smoky restaurant. An ancient woman poured the turbid liquid from a black kettle into our cracked porcelain cups.

Tsarang, the tallest and most inebriated of the yak men, wore black pants cut off at mid-thigh. He offered a toast, "*Dalai Lama, yakbudoo*," and downed the contents of his cup, which the woman promptly refilled. We followed suit. The homemade beer looked like dishwater but was pleasantly bubbly, and it breached the language barrier. We were going to Everest, or "Chomolungma." They were yak men. Each wanted to take us.

As the self-appointed spokesman for the group, Tsarang traced the arc of the sun on the table with his finger three times—three days for the trip to Chomolungma. The other yak men nodded their heads in agreement. Tsarang held up fifteen fingers (fifteen yuan, three U.S. dollars) for himself for each of the three days, and ten fingers each for the two yaks, if burly fingers marching across the table were meant to represent yaks.

"They are cheating you," yelled the Gauloise-smoking Frenchman, who had joined us at the restaurant.

The yak men did not understand the Frenchman's English, but they understood his derogatory tone. John protested that three days was too long; the guidebook said that you could hike from Tingri to Everest in two days. John traced two arcs to Chomolungma. Tsarang shook his head no. I sided with Tsarang. An extra day would help us acclimatize slowly to the change in altitude from 10,000 to 17,000 feet. John stubbornly raised his cup to Chomolungma in two days. Tsarang added a third arc and the yak men laughed.

"He's cheating us," John said when Tsarang ordered another kettle of *chang*.

I reminded John that Tsarang needed an extra day to get his yaks back, and that we did not have a tent or a stove. The yak men laughed when they understood from my tracing of a tent and a stove that we had neither. Tsarang waved them in free. John calculated 105 yuan to be a fair total price for the three days, if it also included kerosene. "And three more for the Dalai Lama," I said, holding up three fingers, invoking 108, Tibetan Buddhism's symbolic number for enlightenment. "Chomolungma, *yakbudoo*," we toasted, and Tsarang refilled our cups.

"You are fools," the Frenchman said.

"Dalai Lama, *yakbudoo*," I said.

"Dalai Lama, *yakbudoo*," the yak men said and touched their cups to their foreheads before downing the *chang*. Tsarang stood up abruptly, mumbled something unintelligible, and left. "He will never come back," the Frenchman told us. Tsarang returned in two hours with a horse cart for our packs. On the way out of town we bought a case of Chinese *pijou* (beer) and a whole quarter of one of Tibet's scrawny sheep. I also plucked a wide-brimmed, beige felt hat off a Tibetan man selling cheap, colorful clothing in front of our hotel. He wanted forty-five yuan but took twenty-five.

"It's filthy," John said, inspecting the sweat-stained brim for infestation.

"Broken in," I corrected.

"Be careful he does not steal everything," the Frenchman yelled after us. I left Tingri thinking that if I were a yak man, I would have stolen the Frenchman's choice food items.

The rain clouds broke and left us standing in a green valley with Cho Oyu lifting the horizon. Cho Oyu was the largest mountain we had ever seen. We could not imagine "knocking the bastard off," as Sir Edmund Hillary said of Everest. Although we had climbed 20,000-foot peaks in Peru, they were mere foothills compared to Cho Oyu's 27,000 feet, and Everest at over 29,000 feet. We were mere inebriated specks in the vast Himalayas.

Tsarang drank only *chang* during our three-day trek. We tried to get him to drink water, but he handed us back beer instead, which we accepted as part of an unwritten social contract. Despite frequent stream crossings and numerous *chang* stops to toast "Dalai Lama, *yakbudoo!*" we crossed the valley in only two hours. Tsarang had the largest house in the village we found there, with hay stacked on its roof as is the custom throughout western Tibet.

There I tried to milk a *dzo* in a corral, to the encouragement of Tsarang's teenage brother, but after milkless minutes the *dzo* kicked me into the dung with its hind foot. Undaunted, I went inside for another yak-byproduct overdose. Tsarang's grandmother looked at us through thick cataracts and asked how much we were paying Tsarang. We mimed the original transaction that led up to 108 fingers. This sent the grandmother into hysterics. Everything we did made her laugh: eating whole boiled potatoes, tossing *tsampa* onto our cheeks instead of into our mouths, dancing with Tsarang while he sang and played a four-string guitar. After a refreshing stop, we were soon back under way again.

"Chuh!" Tsarang yelled at Khampa and Sera, our yaks, who stood motionless and snorted steam from their nostrils in the frigid morning air. "Chuh!" Tsarang yelled again, and threw a softball-sized rock with frightening speed that thumped against Khampa's flank. At each river crossing Khampa tried to buck the case of beer. Sera had the reddish coat and white marking of an Irish Hereford. She had enormous brown eyes and preferred to graze, until a swift kick to the hind quarters made her bolt to the next patch of grass. Such was our skittery introduction to chasing the unruly beasts.

* * *

Dokale was not a town like the map said, but nothing more than two black, yak-hair nomad tents. Unlike these nomad tents, which opened at the top to let the smoke out and fresh air in, Tsarang's ripped, canvas tent let snow in and kept the smoke from escaping. Soon everything we owned smelled like dried rabbit dung, which Tsarang fired red-hot with a bellows under a boiling pot. The smoke, and the sight of John and Tsarang devouring greasy boiled lamb and butter tea, nauseated me. I tried to eat *tsampa* to thwart an impending intestinal eruption. It was too late.

"What are you doing?" I yelled when John poured the water from the boiled lamb into a water bottle.

"Didn't they teach you nutrition in medical school? All the nutrients are in the water. We'll need all the energy we can get."

Seeing the greasy water and bits of lamb in the wide mouth of the water bottle sent me running out of the tent to the nearest hillock. A fine snow covered my tracks by the time I returned, and every other occasion I was forced to sprint from the tent in order to avoid defiling myself. Snow covered our blankets, until daylight illuminated a fairy-land with thick gray clouds and yaks on the hills. That morning it took Tsarang two hours to find Khampa and Sera, who had wandered off in the night. How Tsarang ever found them amazed me. On a distant hill all yaks look alike, and there were hundreds of them. Yaks also do not come when they are called.

Being afflicted with diarrhea in the mountains was infinitely better than having diarrhea in a populated area. The mountains did not care if you dropped your pants while struggling toward a high pass or descending through a valley that narrowed into a gorge. By afternoon the diarrhea, nausea, and a headache made me fall behind Tsarang and the yaks. John stayed close by to humor me through my frequent rest stops.

"Seriously," John said, opening a can of unnaturally pink, greasy meat. "Have some Spam."

• • •

"We've been robbed!" John said when he discovered that our case of Chinese beer was actually nonalcoholic cider. Tsarang had hurried back down the mountain at the onset of a torrential rain, but we had decided to take refuge at what remained of Rombok Monastery. "I paid seventy-five yuan," John lamented. "Twice as much as this cider is worth." I had the worst headache of my life and cared more about avoiding the rain pouring through the slate roof.

A teenage monk in dirty robes entered the room and handed us a thermos of butter tea for which he wanted five yuan, an exorbitant price. Hoping to get rid of him, I paid the money. He proceeded to pull from his robes a freeze-dried shrimp dinner, a can of Cadbury chocolate powder, and an assortment of electrolyte drinks. He insisted that we buy something.

John offered a bottle of cider to the pseudo-lama for the chocolate powder. The monk shook his head no and pointed to the word *pijou* written in Chinese on the case. Of course. The monk did not drink alcohol. John took a sip and demonstrated that we had indeed brought a case of nonalcoholic *pijou*. The monk traded the chocolate for three bottles of cider. Just as John was feeling good about his bargain, the monk demanded ten yuan from each of us for the room.

The rain continued through the evening. We drank cider and moved our sleeping bags to avoid each new leak that sprang in the roof. A reconnaissance of the monastery revealed a solitary, hourglass *stupa* amid the remnants of buildings that had been destroyed during the Cultural Revolution. Sleep was out of the question. John and I stayed awake discussing the ill-fated Everest expedition of Mallory and Irving.

"The climbers in the Mallory expedition used to make fun of the monks at Rombok Monastery," John said. "The monks believed that each rock, plant, and animal on the mountain had its own spirit, and that to disturb anything was to invite death. The British climbers ridiculed the monks for being superstitious and unkempt. The expedition was held up for two months by inclement weather. Finally, the climbers sought the blessing of the old abbot who presided over Rombok. In an ornate ceremony, the abbot pled their case before the ruling spirits. Apparently, the ceremony was not a success; the abbot warned Mallory and Irving that inauspicious portents boded ill for their expedition. But the weather cleared the next day, and the mountaineers were determined to press on. Mallory and Irving climbed to their death."

CHAPTER FOUR

CHOMOLUNGMA, GODDESS MOTHER OF THE WORLD

W E WERE PILGRIMS in a wilderness of catastrophic light and sound. Glacial melt from the Kangshung and East and West Rombok Glaciers thundered through the valley as we hiked the last seven miles from Rombok Monastery in full view of Everest. The snow-covered leviathan appeared weightless. Light bounced off a thousand facets on the mountain ice. Cirrus clouds pulled their fine silk threads across the steep North Face.

We had finally arrived at Everest Base Camp, but we were ill-prepared to stay. Distant tent clusters were the only evidence of life on a moraine criss-crossed by hundreds of gurgling channels. With neither tent nor stove nor extra food, and sneakers and summer sleeping bags instead of hiking boots and winter bags, we offered ourselves like idiots to the elements. Yet this was our challenge; if monks could subsist on barley and water in caves for years, we could scrounge enough food from the pseudo-lamas to hang out a few days at Everest Base Camp.

"We'll offer to carry loads in exchange for food and clothing," John suggested. I reminded John that I was a doctor and that it would not be seemly for me to perform manual work. John failed to see the humor in this and headed toward a far-off group of red and blue tents. I headed toward a separate group of tents beneath a glacier's dirty edge. While imagining the choice food items a well-financed mountaineering expedition might have to offer, I stepped knee-deep into an ice-blue channel.

A sign reading "NO FOOD, KEEP OUT" guarded an enclave of tents, from which fifteen pairs of Japanese glacier goggles eyed the water line on my pants. "How's the weather?" I asked. "No food," said a man bundled in an enormous parka. I introduced myself as an American physician and the same man volunteered that two of their climbers had gotten pulmonary edema. Their doctors were evacuating them to Kathmandu. Daily precipitation had made it too dangerous for their team to get onto the West Ridge. They had tried for one month. I tried to conceal my delight and offered my services. Fifteen pairs of glacier goggles shook their heads no. They had everything they needed. I had the moraine to myself.

I found John next to a similar sign, "NO TREKKERS, NO FOOD!" John had engaged Rod, the base camp manager of an American North Ridge team, in an animated conversation. It turned out that Rod knew Mark Sonnenfeld, our climbing mentor in college, and we took turns recounting epic anecdotes of the young Mark Sonnenfeld being helicopter-rescued in the Canadian Rockies, and breaking his wrist in a fall off Dartmouth's administration building. Clouds suddenly swept Everest from view. "You better set up your tent," Rod said.

"Don't have one," John said. "We were hoping we could carry loads. Blake's a doc."

"*You're* a doc?" Rod said, looking at my wet sneakers and pants. I explained that I had accidentally stepped in a stream, and Rod stuck out his hand in greeting. A Chinese man in his early twenties walked toward us and Rod introduced Mr. Tang, the Chinese Mountaineering Association liaison officer. Rod explained that we were both climbers and would be joining their expedition.

"No more trekkers," Tang said.

"They're *climbers*," Rod replied.

"They not on list," Mr. Tang shouted, becoming red-faced. Rod said that we were staying and Mr. Tang had a tantrum. The more he screamed, the more Rod insisted, until Mr. Tang stomped off toward the Japanese Camp.

"Don't worry about Tang," Rod said as he led us to the team's communal tent. "Tang never agrees to anything. We do what we want." Once inside the tent, it became impossible not to stare at the empty Stroh's beer cans, fruit rolls, bags of hard candy, herb teas, Pepperidge Farm cookies, and an enormous block of cheddar cheese. After weeks of consuming little but yak byproducts, the assortment of junk food seemed irresistible.

"These guys know Sonnenfeld," Rod said when introducing us to Steve, the sickly looking expedition leader, who was sunken into a beach chair next to a radio. He did not offer us any of the food. The radio clicked. "Camp One to Camp Three," Steve said into the receiver.

"Tom at Three. The North Col avalanched this morning. Misha's porters fell 2,000 feet. Hurt bad. One torn knee. One wrenched back. Doubt they'll make it down tonight. Sending Mike with them, over," came the transmission.

"We'll be waiting. Did the yaks arrive? Over."

"Got in a fight with the yak drivers. Their rocks against our ice axes." Sounds of a struggle interrupted the transmission before, "Send *women!*" came screaming through the receiver. Steve jerked the microphone away from his ear.

"Is that you, Strange?"

"I'm so horny the yaks are nervous."

"So is Greg," said Tom's voice, after more wrestling sounds. "He's got diarrhea—I think it's giardia. Send some antibiotics."

Steve looked at us apologetically. "I would carry the medicine up myself, but I pulled an intercostal muscle." Steve demonstrated his wet, hacking cough. Rod said we could "hump" loads for the team and it was agreed. "I'm sending up two trekkers with a load to Camp One tomorrow," Steve said. "Over."

"Do they have nice asses?" came the reply.

Steve saw me staring at a bag of BBQ corn chips and handed me the bag, saying, "Now that you're humping loads, help yourself." Steve explained that Pepperidge Farm cookies were the expedition's favorite, mainly because the company had sent them three times the amount Steve had requested. Ten trekkers who had paid $5,000 each for the privilege had accompanied the team to Base Camp; only one remained. Steve spoke in brief sentence fragments and quickly tired of banter. It had been raining for four weeks. If the rain kept up, they would never get a summit attempt.

"At least we're doing better than the Spanish expedition on the North Face," Rod said. "Poor bastards. They have one of the best Sherpas anywhere. He's summited Everest three times. But it doesn't look like they'll summit." Rod sounded cheerful when he said this.

● ● ●

We joined some of the team members in a hackysack game, in which a circle of players juggle a small, leather sack with their feet without letting it touch the ground. Even Mr. Tang joined in. Tang looked diminutive in his oversized down expedition parka. He scowled at us and often said that he hated mountains. But eventually I grew fond of Mr. Tang. Like any twenty-one-year-old man on his first trip away from home, Mr. Tang longed to return to his family and friends in Beijing. He turned out to be a natural hackysack player. Years of studying martial arts enabled him to send either foot in a roundhouse to retrieve wayward sacks back into the game. The longer we played, the more I admired his skill with his feet.

"He can't play," Mr. Tang said of Yongdup, a bare-chested yak man who strode up to our circle wearing yak-soled boots. Even in his parka, Mr. Tang looked puny next to the well-muscled Yongdup. "He steal water jugs!" Mr. Tang complained. "And cooking pot. You must search his tent."

"Bullshit," Rod said, and tossed the tiny leather sack to Yongdup. Yongdup kicked the sack twenty yards into the moraine. "You can't trust him!" Mr. Tang shrieked. Yongdup stepped up to within inches of Tang's face. Mr. Tang had no concept of compromise, which left him in jeopardy of either losing face in an argument or else being beaten up by Yongdup. John distracted Yongdup by retrieving the sack and lobbing it back to him. Again, Yongdup kicked the sack defiantly back into the scree. There was no limit to Yongdup's laughter, just as there was no getting him to play by our rules.

● ● ●

The next morning I got up early with Brack, a cardiothoracic surgeon who was part of the team, in order to examine the two Sherpas injured in the avalanche the day before, who were now lying quietly in a tent across the moraine. One man had a grotesquely swollen knee. The right side of the other man's back was tender and swollen. The Sherpas were incredible. They had fallen 2,000 feet in an avalanche and then walked fourteen miles down a glacier.

"They're lucky to be alive," Brack said, with the confidence of a man who himself had participated in eight Himalayan expeditions. He gave the men some pain pills and directions in Nepalese. Outside the tent, Brack said, "The older man has a grade-four tear of the medial collateral ligament in his right knee. Unless he gets an operation in Kathmandu, he'll never climb again. But he can't afford to go to Kathmandu. Maybe it's just as well—the operation also could do him more harm than good."

Brack smiled when I asked him if he had seen many cases of pulmonary and cerebral edema, where in reaction to shifts in altitude the lungs or brain become engorged with fluid. "I've never seen a single case," he said. "I guess I'm lucky."

* * *

John and I met Misha on the terminal moraine in full view of Everest. We were in a tremendous mood. Rod had loaned us down sleeping bags rated to forty degrees below zero. We would be carrying a load to Camp One tomorrow, which meant that we would be eating with the team for the indefinite future. And the music of the Doors was blaring on the largest cassette box we had ever seen.

Talking to Rod, we learned he was an amiable wealth of information about the three American teams on Everest that season. A British climber named Doug Scott was leading an expedition that was expected any day. They would try the Northeast Ridge, where the British climbers Joe Tasker and Pete Boardman had disappeared at 27,000 feet in 1982. As with their legendary countrymen Mallory and Irving, their bodies had never been recovered. "Shit," Rod said, noticing a man with a mane of unkempt Medusa hair bounding toward us across the expanse of moraine. This was our first glimpse of Misha.

Misha had wild, eccentric blue eyes. He walked to within inches of Rod's face before screaming, "I not paying Sherpas. They are laziest goddamned Sherpas I ever had."

Rod looked Misha directly in the eye and said, "You're lucky they didn't get killed in that avalanche."

Misha clenched his fists and yelled, "Sherpas lie. There was no avalanche! Sherpas steal my cameras! Sherpas steal everything." Misha turned to John and said, "I am Misha, famous Russian filmmaker. Maybe you see one of my mountain films on German television?" Misha snapped his head back to Rod and softened his tone. "I need to use your ropes."

"Why did you send your Sherpas up in an avalanche?" Rod asked.

"I lose all my equipment because of fucking Sherpas."

"You can't use our ropes," Rod said.

I thought Misha would punch Rod, but he stormed across the moraine like a spoiled child in the direction of his tents. "You'll never meet nicer people than these Sherpas," Rod said, as Misha stomped away. "They're honest. They do most of the dangerous climbing on most Himalayan expeditions. Misha doesn't do any hard climbing. He sends his Sherpas to fix all of his lines before he goes up. We don't have any Sherpas. We want to do everything ourselves."

● ● ●

At sixty-five years old, Charlie was the expedition's youngest spirit. We hiked with him to Camp One, at 18,000 feet, where one of the climbers from Camp Three would come down from 21,500 feet to ferry more choice food items back up to where the expedition was beginning its technical climbing. Charlie's white, Santa Claus hair and beard gave away his age; Buddy, his mountaineering teddy bear, dressed in its own miniature wool pants, down parka, and glacier goggles and strapped on top of Charlie's pack, belied it. After Rod finished packing our loads, we learned that twenty-five pounds felt twice as heavy at this altitude as it did in the flatlands.

As the three of us started across the moraine, Charlie stuttered, "Well 'B-Buddy, are you r-ready?" I wondered if Charlie always trekked with his teddy bear, or if the altitude had done this to him. He told John and me, "You go right ahead, gentlemen. I'll hike slower than both of you. Don't wait for me."

"We wouldn't think of hiking without you," John said. John wasn't threatened by Charlie's talking to Buddy, but I couldn't help thinking that there must have been something wrong with a grown man who consulted his teddy bear before each drink of water, snack, or rest. Hiking at my own pace in front of Charlie and John, I questioned Charlie's sanity as the trail wound through house-sized boulders and tall dirt columns sculpted by rain and runoff. Everest disappeared from view once the trail turned up a side valley that carried the East Rombok Glacier. I should have waited for John and Charlie, but I was impatient and hiked ahead.

Endless switchbacks wound ever higher above the trickle of glacial melt sparkling in the sun. As my heart beat louder and my mind moved slower, fear tugged at the base of my brain. Was my body acclimatizing quickly enough to compensate for the changes in altitude? Was water oozing through my alveolar membranes to fill my lungs with pulmonary edema? Was my brain swelling like a wet sponge to herniate against the base of my skull? The symptoms of Acute Mountain Sickness summed up how I felt at the moment: headache, dizziness, nausea, no desire to eat or drink. I collapsed to rest when I arrived at a cairn of rocks. A marmot barked at my approach. Charlie and John arrived with a refreshing breeze that blew cool air off the end of the glacier.

* * *

At Camp One, Tom, Steve's radio correspondent, bounded off the ice and immediately gulped down two liters of the grape drink we had brought. Between gulps, Tom told us that he had hiked down from Camp Three, approximately ten miles, in just over two hours. With luck, he would make it back to Three in time for dinner. Tom had just finished his internship in Seattle, where he had arranged to postpone his residency in anesthesiology until January so he could go on this expedition. For future reference, I asked how he had finagled a break between internship and residency. "Ever hear of the Hornbine Couloir on Everest?" Tom said. "Well, the famous Hornbine happens to be my residency director."

Tom filled his pack with our loads and, before stepping onto the glacier, handed me a stamped letter from his back pocket. "I almost forgot. Would you mind giving this to Rod? It's a letter to my wife and kids."

"R-Ready, B-Buddy?" Charlie asked, as he prepared to join Tom on the hike back up to Camp Three, and I thought how precious the human body is, how delicate the balance between life and death.

With Tom and Charlie gone, John and I ate as much of the expedition food as we could. We deserved it after carrying our loads. Triscuits and sardines with mustard sauce naturally led to potato chips and cheddar cheese and quarts of grape drink, granola bars, mixed nuts, raisins, and fruit rolls. I ate so much my stomach felt full for the first time in over a month. Without warning, the stream five hundred feet below suddenly seemed noticeably louder. I shortly thereafter succumbed to four bouts of projectile vomiting.

"Hold still!" John yelled, hurrying to position his camera. "O.K. Now do it again."

* * *

Back at Base Camp later that evening, Yongdup unzipped the door of the communal tent and stepped brazenly inside, accompanied by two yak men who gawked at the incredible array of food and equipment. Their smiles reminded me of my own first sight of the tent. "No," Rod said to Yongdup, who was helping himself to a bag of pretzels. "No," to one yak man, who found a bottle of rice wine. A still louder "No!" to the other yak man, who grabbed a case of Pepperidge Farm cookies. Suddenly the three men turned on Rod. I was afraid for myself and pushed my beach chair against the wall of the tent. Rod traded handfuls of pretzels in exchange for the rice wine and cookies, and herded the yak men out. "Expeditions breed this kind of relationship," Rod said.

* * *

Two days later, cough or no cough, Steve was determined to get to Camp Three. Rod hiked slowly with Steve. If all went well, Charlie would be waiting to meet us at Camp Two, and would then return to Base Camp with us. John and I did not know the route to Camp Two, but we did not want to wait for Rod and Steve. A trail of sticks with red plastic flags led us back onto the lip of the East Rombok Glacier. We moved cautiously around holes in the ice, beneath which a freezing river raged through dark caverns. We took care to see that the other was not getting too tired or had lost his sense of humor, early warning signs of altitude sickness.

I got a headache that afternoon. John tried to get me to eat more sardines, the idea of which made both of us laugh until our stomachs hurt. A trail zig-zagged across the glacier to a steep scree slope on one side of the valley, then back to the other side. The sun had slickened the icy jaws of the trail that opened into the river. Twice great sprays of rocks and car-sized boulders rained down from the cathedrals of rotten stone at the valley's rim. Twice we sprinted in terror before realizing that we were a safe distance away. The higher we climbed, the thicker the glacier became, until the ice beneath our feet was hundreds of feet thick. As the valley narrowed and steepened, the glacier threw countless creaking ice pinnacles into the path of the wind. We were insects in a giant's world. The higher we climbed, the smaller and more insignificant we became.

One foot fell in front of the other. Thoughts acquired a weight of their own: the Sherpa's discombobulated knee; climbers fighting the yak men; Rod fighting with Misha; everyone fighting with Mr. Tang. Mountains emphasize the best and the worst in each of us.

Camp Two's tents sat on their own ridge of lateral moraine, a safe distance from avalanches, dwarfed beneath vertical oceans of scree and the energetic sweep of the glacier. Charlie cradled Buddy like a nursing baby. "B-B-Buddy and I are g-glad to s-see you," he said. He looked tired but he talked enthusiastically about the North Col, where the Sherpas had been avalanched off the mountain. In the morning Rod wasn't feeling well and decided to hike back down to Base Camp with Charlie, John, and myself. A rejuvenated Steve climbed alone to Camp Three.

* * *

We took three days to recuperate from humping loads to Camp Two. Then tragedy struck again. We met death in a boulder field. A solemn procession of Japanese climbers with glacier glasses and zinc oxide over their sun-charred faces carried a corpse lashed to a stretcher of ski poles.

Twenty-four climbers followed. The funeral procession passed as quickly as it had come, and I found myself wanting to know how the climber had died, as though knowing would help me avoid a similar situation.

"I've never seen a dead body," John said, resting on a boulder. "My grandfather had a closed casket. No one else in my family has died."

I told John about an autopsy I had done on a man who had left a bar without paying and driven at high speed into a tree. The car exploded and burned for half an hour before the firemen could pull him out. I couldn't even identify the man's race; his cooked flesh smelled sweet, like barbecue.

"That's disgusting," John said.

"He had *liters* of beer in his stomach. Smelling *that* was disgusting."

"You sound so removed," John said. "How old were you when your dad died? *That* must have been hard on you."

I had seen my father die from lung cancer when I was fourteen, then a close friend drown the following spring. Eventually I'd seen several friends die in climbing accidents, and many people die in hospitals. John wondered if the climber had a wife and children, if there was a God who cared about each of us, if one of us would get hurt. I told him that we were cosmic fertilizer.

* * *

The next day, a group of yak men loaded their shaggy beasts and beat them into a line across the moraine long before the sun had chiseled the prehistoric chill from the valley floor. John was carrying two fifteen-pound oxygen bottles. I carried a twenty-five-pound tape deck and five pounds of batteries. Rod filled his pack with choice food items. Once the yaks hit the switchbacks, it would be too dangerous to try to pass all fifteen of the behemoths. With no incentive to catch up, we took frequent rests. Hiking slowly would give our bodies more time to acclimatize and help us avoid getting sick during the fourteen-mile hike from Base Camp to Camp Three. If all went well, we would stay at Camp Two that night, and continue to Camp Three tomorrow.

On a switchback above us, a yak bucked a blue barrel that careened down a steep dirt embankment toward the river. As the barrel tumbled faster down the slope, I hoped that it didn't contain anything choice, like Pepperidge Farm cookies. I did not see the ton of charging mane and horns until it was upon me. "Chuh!" I shrieked, and threw a rock at the yak. The beast kept coming and I leapt off the trail after the barrel.

An unfamiliar yak man ran down the trail after me. He pretended to throw a baseball-sized rock at my head. Only then did I realize that the yaks were from the Spanish team coming down, not from our North Ridge team going up. The yak man had seen me throwing a rock at his yak, and blamed me for his load bounding toward the river. He looked crazed, like he wanted to kill me. I ran far enough down the slope that John became an easier target.

"*Tashi delek*," John said, "*To te che*" (thank you), his hands folded as if in prayer. The yak man pretended to throw the rock at his head. "Hello-thank you," John pleaded and pointed to me, "He did it."

• • •

A loud *CLAP* came from the rotten amphitheater of cliffs a thousand feet above us. *CLAP-CLAP* and our heads snapped up to see yak-sized boulders careening off an ancient buttress. The boulders seemed to fall for a long time before they hit the shoulder of scree, and exploded into perfect waves of shattered rock that fanned toward us. The expanding waves seduced us with their beauty, this glimpse of death. We ran from them as much for fun as from any real danger.

At Camp Two, Brack and another climber drank soup outside their tents. Brack looked pale. His eyes were sunken and listless. He introduced us to Paul, a short, stocky man who spilled Knorr leek and potato soup into his beard. "Paul got pulmonary edema during the night," Brack said authoritatively, even though he looked worse than Paul. "He's doing well now. As soon as we finish our soup, we'll continue to Base Camp."

"It's funny," Paul said. "Last night I woke up drowning in my own juice. Now I'm drinking soup."

"I didn't need a stethoscope to diagnose this one," Brack said. "Paul got better with sitting up and oxygen. I didn't have to use Lasix. We hiked down at daylight. With a bit of luck, we'll make it to Base Camp in time for dinner." Brack spent all of his breath talking and paused to sip his soup. Paul looked sternly at Brack, who grudgingly continued, "That's only half of it. This morning I vomited bright red blood, twice."

"I'm going with you," Rod said.

"That won't be necessary," Brack said.

"It's mountain etiquette," Rod said. "I grew up in the mountains. It will get dark before you get off the glacier."

"We'll be fine," Brack said gruffly, and wobbled to his tent.

Bad judgment is a classic sign of mountain sickness, something climbers have to be vigilant for in themselves and their partners at all times. I followed Brack to a rock with a view of the ice sails billowing down the frozen river in front of us. I was a recent graduate from medical school with no independent experience, and Brack was a cardiothoracic surgeon and veteran of eight Himalayan expeditions. All of this made me hesitate before saying the obvious: Brack had a bleeding ulcer and was too stubborn to admit it. He did not speak for some time and appeared to be in the throes of indecision. "We'll make it to Base Camp tonight," Brack said. "The question in my mind is whether I should go straight to the American Hospital in Kathmandu. I don't want to go."

"You have two choices," I said. "You can stay in Base Camp and worry. Or you can do what you would tell one of your patients to do."

• • •

That night, alone at Camp Two, John and I listened eagerly to the evening's radio communication. "Rod at Base to Three, over."

"Tom at Three. How's Paul?"

"Paul's lungs are clear. He's eating soup and loving it. Brack's resting in his tent. He didn't vomit any more blood. I did orthostatics on him. He's fine, just tired."

"Glad to hear it. We're all rooting for him. Will he evacuate to Kathmandu?"

"Doesn't want to."

"Have the Japanese doc look at him tonight."

"Already did."

"Good job," Tom said. "I'm sleeping by the radio tonight. I'll turn the radio on every two hours for one minute. Call if there's a problem.

Everyone carried full loads to Camp Four today. If the weather holds, we'll establish Camp Five next week."

"Here's the latest on the Japanese death," Rod said. "He was their best climber. He was exhausted, descending from 23,000 feet to rest at Base, and drowned crossing the river."

Vertical oceans of scree and the energetic sweep of the glacier dwarfed Camp Two's tents. John won the toss for Rod's expedition sleeping bag and slept soundly. I spent the night shivering in everything I had: thermodactyl long underwear, warm-up pants, Carolyn's silk top, a wool sweater and wool pants, balaclava, three pairs of socks, and two summer sleeping bags. John and I had experienced many sleepless nights in snow caves, on cliff ledges, in boxcars, and on the side of the road. Shivering as Orion crawled across the sky, I realized that for the first time since I had arrived in the mountains, I felt healthy.

Snowfall obliterated the trail to Camp Three. The morning's radio communication confirmed "heavy dumping." As Yongdup broke camp and drove the yaks ever farther up the glacier, we spent the day playing rummy and foraging through Camp Two's extensive cache of peanut M&M's, Cadbury chocolate, and quarts of hot Jello, vegetable soup, and macaroni and cheese.

At noon, we ventured onto the folds of Changtse's Glacier. We explored wind tunnels and climbed flying buttresses of blue ice. A bare-handed ascent up the back of a gently sloping serac led to an adrenaline-filled descent through feathery crust. That night we gorged ourselves on junk food and played rummy for six hours. I slept soundly in Rod's expedition bag.

Carrying our packs even a short distance the next morning gave fresh insight into the climber's expression, "humping loads." I sang songs in my head, even songs that I hated, to keep myself from going insane with boredom as the spectacular ice highway turned into an endless series of rises. This eventually led to cursing in foreign languages: *"Ya kelb, yebne kelb"* ("You dog, son of a dog," in Egyptian); *"Ta tum kalooch. T'un pisc que ho disc. Vay ood jarack varie"* ("Squash head. You're not wearing any underwear. You smell horrible," in Armenian); *"Va tu faire foutre, grand merde"* ("Go fuck yourself, big shit," in French); and *"Como caca. No come las uvas"* ("Eat shit, don't eat the grapes," in Spanish). Even John looked mad. "Fuck Everest," I said to the Northeast Ridge that unfolded before us for hours without end. "Fuck climbing," I said to the fresh snowfall. "Fuck," I said to myself, 1,008 times.

• • •

We swaggered into Camp Three with the Doors blaring on the tape deck at peak volume. John and I thought it made for an appropriate way to introduce ourselves to the expedition members we hadn't met yet. It took several minutes for the climbers to crawl from their tents.

"You made great time," said Steve, whose cough had gotten worse. "Looking good," said Tom, the expedition's remaining doc. "Let's party," said the other Steve, who everyone referred to as "Strange." We remembered him from our first radio transmission—he was the one who'd inquired about the comeliness of our asses. Strange sang along with us to Jim Morrison, "Break on through. Break on through. Break on through. *YEAAAA-AHHHH!*"

It must have been Strange's ebullient nature that inspired me to add a quarter-cup of fresh black pepper, ginger, cinnamon, and ten cloves of garlic into that night's meal, a salmon curry. Jeff, the only Canadian on the team, talked incessantly with us about how many loads everyone had carried and how their performance related to their chances of gaining the summit. He also put out the fires when kerosene dripping from the Nepalese stove ignited. "Pete summited Everest once from the Nepalese side," Jeff said. "He's strong as a yak. So is Tom, but he's the only doc left and has to stay low. That leaves four out of ten who've been able to hump loads to Camp Four. Greg tried once and left his pack on the ridge. Do you believe that? A real sap. Mike's a businessman. He hasn't carried a load yet. But he donated $40,000 to the expedition. He can climb with me anytime."

Once eleven people were crammed into Camp Three's smaller version of Base Camp's communal tent, Strange announced, "This curry's hot enough to burn the ass hairs off a yak. I like it." All of the climbers who had humped loads to Camp Four agreed.

"It's too hot for me," Greg said. Those who had not carried loads nodded.

"It's time for the game you've all been waiting for," Strange announced, and then pulled his knees to his chest to accentuate his rear. "'The Lowest Common Social Denominator.'"

"Take cover," Pete yelled and pulled his fishing hat over his face.

Ripples of discontent erupted from the non-load carriers as Strange lit a match and sang, "*Break on through!*" He held the match to his backside, and an instant later a jackhammer fart belched orange flames from his rear.

"That's disgusting," Greg said.

"The yak men almost killed us," Strange told John and me. His bushy black eyebrows quivered as he recounted how Yongdup had refused to drive the yaks the last thousand meters to Camp Three. A shouting match between the yak men and the climbers escalated into a battle. The yak men armed themselves with rocks. The climbers clutched their ice axes nervously. Luckily, no one got hurt. For an extra ten dollars, the yak men agreed to drive the yaks the remaining distance. John recounted our own epic conflict with the yak men from the Spanish team.

"I'd like to go down to Base Camp tomorrow and rest," Mike said. "But with the route going up so fast, I'm afraid to be away. I might miss the summit."

"Don't strain yourself worrying," Strange warned. "We hardly have Camp Four established. It's a long way to Six." Strange turned to the man with the fishing hat. "Goddamnit, Pete. If you hump loads any faster we'll get heart attacks trying to keep up."

"I can't believe Misha sent his Sherpas to fix the North Col with heavy avalanche danger," Pete said. "It had snowed for three days straight. Those men are better climbers than all of us put together. Misha sent them to their death."

"I say we disembowel Misha and feed him to the vultures," Strange said. "And Tang. That son of a bitch fought us every step of the way. He was a nightmare flying our gear from Beijing to Lhasa. Chop them both into little bits. We'll have a Tibetan sky burial."

I had seen pictures of a Tibetan sky burial: people hacking flesh from human corpses and mixing it with *tsampa* to feed to the vultures. Like us, the expedition members unanimously despised China's destruction of Tibetan culture, just as the United States had exterminated native American cultures. But here we were, subsidizing China's occupation of

Tibet with our tourist dollars. Eating salmon curry and Pepperidge Farm cookies in enormous expedition sleeping bags on the slopes of Everest, Tibet seemed light-years away.

"I'm going to Antarctica next year," Greg said. "I want to be the youngest person in the world to climb the highest mountain on each continent. I've already got North and South America and Africa. Antarctica is easy. But it costs $12,000 for the air fare from Patagonia to Antarctica. The airline has a monopoly. Anybody want to come?"

"Hand me the cough medicine," Strange bellowed. "A toast to Brack, the concocter of this medieval brew."

"Give it to me next," Greg said.

"Don't let Mike have any," Strange said. "He's addicted." Mike did not say anything. Codeine, I learned, after taking a sweet vermilion sip, was the anti-tussive ingredient Brack had used in mixing up this home remedy—enough codeine for my mind to feel unsteady in my body when I tried to fall asleep in the warm expedition bag.

* * *

The next morning I crawled out of the tent not knowing if I were going to vomit or defecate. I felt dizzy. A pounding headache made it impossible to appreciate my first view of the North Col's 3,000-foot curtain of ice and a foreshortened view of the summit. John made me eat Fig Newtons with powdered milk and I soon felt well enough to hike to the top of the East Rombok Glacier. Jeff pointed to the team's fixed ropes up to the ridge, then the two miles of ridge to Camp Four, illustrating how camps Five and Six were weeks away. Their approach to the summit through the steppes was clear of snow, thanks to the jet stream scouring the rock clean with 200-mile-an-hour winds.

A cornice broke off the rim of the North Col above us and blossomed into a spindrift avalanche. I held my breath. There was nowhere to run. The avalanche was miles away, but distances were deceiving. Jeff pointed out where the Sherpas fell from the North Col, then looked longingly at the summit. "I'm twenty-two years old. I'll never be in better shape. I want the summit. You've got to want it. I want it bad."

* * *

Rod looked well when we passed him on the glacier below Camp Two. Tom, Greg, and Mike were coming down with us to Base Camp for a rest. We joked with Rod that he should treat himself to an extra day at Camp Two. Rod insisted that he could make it from Base Camp to Camp Three in two days. This was fast, going from 17,000 to 21,500 feet, but Rod had just carried a load to 19,500 feet without problems. Then, the next day, he missed the morning radio call. At noon a barely audible voice was heard asking for help. It took precious minutes for us to discern that Rod had awoken with a "killer" headache. He had not been able to see or move for hours.

"What have you done so far?" Tom asked.

"I crawled to the oxygen tank. I took a Fiorinol. My headache's a little better."

Tom looked at each of us to see if we understood that Rod had cerebral edema, and his brain was being squashed against his skull. "No wonder his headache feels better," Tom said with the receiver off. "He took a narcotic." Clicking back on, he said, "Keep nursing the oxygen. How's your vision?"

"Better."

"Who else is in Three?"

"Just me. Everyone left to carry loads to Four."

"Jesus," Tom yelled again with the receiver off. "How do five people leave camp and not see that Rod could die any moment?" Click: "You're going to be fine, Rod. It sounds like the worst is over. Hike down when they get back. Bring someone with you. There's oxygen at Two. We'll talk again in one hour."

That night Rod and Steve arrived in Base Camp in time for another gourmet treat: pressure-cooked turnips sauteed with onions and cabbage and too much fresh black pepper (but never too much garlic), topped with a roux of yak cheese and powdered milk. A sumptuous feast in celebration of Rod's being alive.

"This is fantastic!" Rod said, smacking his lips. "I'm not a religious man, but I thank God last night is over. I had the most intense headache of my life. I tried to call for help but I couldn't move. I couldn't see or hear. By morning everyone had left to hump a load. I couldn't call out. I knew I had cerebral edema."

"We were worried about you," Tom said.

Rod laughed. "I was worried about me, too."

* * *

A clanking reverberated across the moraine from a convoy of Chinese Army trucks, which had brought generators, gravel, steel, and a small army of tents. "Chinese expedition," Tang said proudly, and described how the construction of new cement platforms was only the beginning. Concession stands would be completed within the year.

"Another humongous Chinese assault on Everest," Rod said. "In 1960, the Chinese attacked Everest from Tibet with 214 people. They claimed that three climbers made it to the summit. But they did it at night, and couldn't take a picture."

"Three Chinese climbers made the summit," Tang shouted. Rod said that the Nepalese were so mad at China for trying to appropriate their holy mountain that Gurkha soldiers with fixed bayonets lined the road all the way from the airport to the city when the Chinese Premier arrived in Kathmandu. "Three climbers made the summit," Mr. Tang shouted again.

Rod and Mr. Tang continued to argue against the backdrop of the clanking generators. As much as I had been enjoying our encounter with the American Everest team, I longed to return to Lhasa. I began to focus on the garbage surrounding us, abandoned by hundreds of previous expeditions: piles of rusty cans, broken bottles, batteries, medical waste, and high-tech plastics with a half-life of 100,000 years, all tucked in middens across the terminal moraine.

Two days later we paid 150 yuan each to a Tibetan truck driver who took us to the main road. It was an exorbitant price, but we were too tired for the two-day walk. Crammed into an open truck with a dozen other trekkers, I contemplated the unanswered questions left in my mind after our encounter with the North Ridge expedition. Would Brack hemorrhage on the way to the hospital in Kathmandu? Would any of the climbers make it to the summit? What would the world's highest concession stands do to Everest Base Camp?

PART TWO

SKY BURIAL

CHAPTER FIVE

THE FORBIDDEN CITY

RIDING BACK TO Lhasa, I saw young lovers sitting in a field of purple nycothiums. They reminded me of Carolyn. So did the Tibetan women spreading barley out to dry. I wondered if Carolyn was still in Lhasa, and if she had missed me during our month-long excursion into the mountains. The driver kicked us out at the edge of a desolate valley. We shouted obscenities at him when he drove off. We did not realize our mistake until we walked around a small hill that had concealed the Xegar checkpoint from view; if the driver had been caught with passengers, he could have been fined and lost his license.

Two unarmed guards stood at the checkpoint. Confident that we were unrecognizably dirty, we walked past the guards toward the adjacent truck stop. The guards shouted after us, but then retired to their hut. We wanted food and our first showers in a month, but we soon learned that the truck stop had not had food for a week and that it could spare us no more than a thermosful of hot water. John opened a map and a can of Chinese Spam. He held up a chunk of smoked pink flesh and made a toast: "In the spirit of epic adventure, may Everest pale compared to our next and even greater expedition."

Two German men in their thirties were waiting on the Lhasa side of the checkpoint. Hans had a crew cut and wisps of blond beard. He looked like a young Anagarika Govinda, the German monk whose decades-long pilgrimage through Tibet, as recounted in his book *The Way of the White Clouds*, explored Tibetan Buddhism's spiritual horizons. His friend Otto had stringy, shoulder-length hair and a penetrating gaze. "We come from Kathmandu," Otto said. "The border is shit. Three days we hike across landslides. More than a hundred people die this monsoon season." Otto spoke in German to Hans and they laughed. "It is unfortunate only twelve tourists die, and no Americans," he translated for John and me. John liked Otto's defiant attitude, but I was leery of him. He had the demeanor of a Khampa, which made me wary of my valuables.

A rising plume of dust on the horizon streaked toward us. Watching the approaching dust devil, I imagined a monk bounding across the 12,000-foot plateau in effortless, exaggerated strides. In Tibet some monks are known to cover large distances at superhuman speeds. While I believed that such things were possible, I was not surprised to see a bus materialize at the head of the dust plume. It took two hours for the guards to check everyone's passports and let the bus through. When the bus finally pulled up in front of us, I assumed it was to pick us up. I did not see its flat tire. Otto pushed past an ashen man fighting to get out of the bus in order to vomit. A horrible smell accompanied the gauntlet of harsh stares from other passengers as John and I headed toward the two remaining seats in the back.

"Whuh," I gagged at chunks of dried vomit in a topographical relief on the seat. John's suggestion that we clean it up brought more harsh stares from the passengers who had sat next to the mess. Outside in the fresh air I realized there was no way I could get back on the bus. Even if we didn't get sick trying to clean the seat, we would have to endure that smell for the days it would take us to get from Xegar to Lhasa.

Just then an army jeep skidded to a halt at the checkpoint. The driver was Tibetan. A PLA soldier sat in the passenger side. I said hello in Tibetan and Chinese: "*Tashi delek*" and "*Ni hao*," and asked, "Lhasa?" The driver nodded. I ran back into the bus, and found John's face hostage to the same contortion as the other passengers. "Fuck America," Otto yelled out the bus window after us as we climbed into the jeep.

John handed a pack of Marlboro cigarettes to the front of the jeep for Tenzin, the driver, who never smiled, and Zheng, the soldier, whose uniform was two sizes too big. Tenzin threw the wrapper out the window and accelerated onto the dirt road. Just as I was beginning to fantasize about reaching Lhasa and having a hot bath, the jeep hit a pothole that shot us against the roof. The joy of having a 360-degree view of the mountains faded as Tenzin barreled over and into more potholes.

The jeep broke down regularly. Fortunately, Tenzin was a mechanical wizard. He replaced an old alternator belt with a larger one from a tractor in a nearby village. Dust in the fuel line was sucked by mouth out of the tube. Radiator leaks were plugged with a rag. The jeep broke down so many times that I stopped counting after twenty.

I think Zheng tried to tell us his life story, but neither John nor I spoke enough Chinese to understand him. Like Mr. Tang, the Everest expedition's liaison officer, Zheng was in his early twenties and hated mountains. He had been stationed in Tibet for several years and longed to return to the mainland. He also disliked Tibetans, which explained why Tenzin never smiled.

Rain the second day made the jeep stick fast in the muck in addition to breaking down. We became covered in mud after wedging stones under the wheels and pushing it out of ruts. Then Tenzin drove forty miles an hour off the road. Miraculously, no one was hurt. With oil, water, and gas leaks, we broke down every fifteen minutes. I stopped counting after fifty.

Ironically, we ran out of gas twenty-five miles from Lhasa. Many army trucks passed us, but none would stop for the Tibetan driver, for the Chinese soldier, or for the American who yelled "Fuck you" at receding taillights. At first I was angry that we would have to spend one more night outside. I noticed that the electricity lines that paralleled the road did not branch up to a nearby Tibetan village. Tibetan homes were lit by butter lamps, as they had been for centuries; they had neither electricity nor showers. At dawn Zheng flagged a driver who let us siphon enough gas to get to Lhasa.

* * *

The well-dressed tourists at the Lhasa Hotel's main desk eyed us suspiciously. I explained to the manager that we had just come from Everest. He smiled uneasily, but he took my American Express card. We took two baths each and still could not wash the blue dye from our cheap pants off our legs. John looked thin; he had lost ten pounds. I was emaciated, having lost twenty-five. We ate five meals in a row without leaving the premises: copious amounts of stainless steel eggs and cold toast, overcooked yak burgers and greasy fries, beef stroganoff and sugary desserts. The food didn't taste very good but we wanted to satisfy our cravings for Western cooking before we resettled in a Tibetan hotel.

"Are you staying *here?*" Otto shouted when he discovered us in the lobby. Otto and Hans sported a motley assemblage of dirt that offended the sensibilities of the hotel's refined clientele—the same dirt that had covered us less than twenty-four hours before. "The Lhasa Hotel is fucked," Otto bellowed, loud enough to attract the manager's attention. John said we were leaving. Otto berated us "soft Americans" for taking a luxurious jeep while he stayed on the bus.

"Change money for me," Otto demanded. "I lose my passport." Otto retrieved a 500-mark note from a sack hung around his neck. I took the bill to the main desk and the manager said that German marks had to be changed at the bank. Otto glared at me and shouted, "They would change American dollars. Chinese treat Tibetans like shit. FEC's (foreign exchange currency) are fucked. The Lhasa Hotel is fucked."

Lhasa had changed since we had left a month before. Squads of police goose-stepped in the streets while roving loudspeakers denounced the Dalai Lama as an enemy of the Motherland. It took two days for me to find a letter from Carolyn on the Tibetan hotel bulletin board. She had stayed for another two weeks after her brother returned from Kham, then went on to Nepal. She would be at the Tibet Hotel in Kathmandu.

Otto was soon arrested for stealing a government stamp. After a policeman refused to authorize a special visa to Bhutan, Otto stole the government stamp. No one witnessed the theft, but when Otto returned from his trip and heard that the police had searched his room, he gave himself up. For five days no one knew what had happened to him. Even I began to miss him. Then Otto reappeared one evening at a Chinese restaurant.

"I was in Drapchi Prison," Otto announced.

"Did they beat you?" John asked seriously.

"It was like a hotel!" Otto said. "I had my own room. In the morning, the guard asked me what I wanted to eat, then sent someone to the market. The guards were O.K. until the last day. The bastards charged me forty FEC." John asked if Otto had seen any other prisoners. Otto said that he had not.

"Was it worth it?" John asked.

"I gave government back their stamp," Otto said, "but first I make two visas."

* * *

"We have to see the Potala," John said once we had settled into the third floor of the Banak Shol Hotel. "That is, *if* you can handle being a tourist for a few hours." John put a colorful, postcard-sized sticker of the Tibetan national flag on his black shoulder bag. I admired the colorful sticker of two facing snow lions with red and blue rays streaming from a rising sun. John gave me one. He had gotten two at the Office of Tibet in New York, and had forgotten about them until now. I put the sticker on the cover of my journal. We rented bicycles from the hotel and raced them through the streets to the Potala Palace.

I had imagined that the Potala's thousand small rooms would be adorned with *thankas* that portrayed alternately enlightened or horrific manifestations of the human subconscious against a backdrop of colorful silk brocade, with the walls blackened by eons of accumulated soot and floors slippery from centuries of spilled yak butter. John veered his bicycle around a dog with a mutilated haunch that stared at two men unloading yak quarters from the back of a truck onto the dirt alley.

At the palace we locked our bicycles and walked up the long switchback of stairs; dwarfed by the palace's white walls rising into a cobalt sky, I thought of standing at the base of Half Dome in Yosemite with John three years ago. We had climbed the Northwest Buttress in one day instead of the usual two. In order to lighten our loads we did not bring extra equipment or clothing. We carried one quart of water each during the eleven-hour ascent, and each lost fifteen pounds. A lightning storm approached the cliff as we summited, and we ran down the back of the dome without touching the metal handrail.

Six Chinese soldiers with AK-47s slung over their shoulders smoked cigarettes at the entrance. I wondered if the police were there to arrest the monks for subversive activity. Surely they were not sightseeing. "*Tashi delek*," I greeted the soldiers in Tibetan. They did not respond. We paid our entrance fees and passed through a large wooden gate into a courtyard with red and green trim on the wooden balcony.

A Chinese woman standing on the steps leading into the Potala's East Wing spoke to a tour in English. "Before Tibet's peaceful liberation from its feudal past," the woman said, "serfs had no rights. Brutal warlord monks tortured their serfs in human sacrifices. Now, thanks to the People's Government, the monks at the Potala Palace enjoy total religious freedom. I have arranged for you to meet a Tibetan monk who will tell you how happy the Tibetans are in the Motherland."

"These Tibetans are barbaric," an overweight man said. He was breathing hard and had the crimson face and distended neck veins that precede a massive coronary. John and I looked at each other in stunned disbelief; no one had questioned the tour guide's version of Tibetan history.

I noticed a beckoning side door next to the stairs that was slightly ajar. The soldiers had entered the courtyard but were not paying attention to the tour. John saw me moving toward the door and grinned enthusiastically. Without saying anything, we walked through the side door. Shouts followed us down a corridor that opened into rooms piled with carpenters' tools and stacks of slate shingles. The voices almost caught up to us as an unlocked wooden door led us into a red courtyard. There were no visible handholds on the steep maroon walls. A half-wall on one side looked out over the valley floor 500 feet below. We were trapped. The voices were upon us.

Terrified of being caught, I climbed over the half-wall, lowered myself gently onto a two-foot-wide slate roof, and crawled as fast as I could beneath the locked wooden shutters that lined the wall. John followed. No soldiers ventured onto the roof after us, but I continued to crawl farther away from the yelling. The houses on the valley floor looked diminutive next to the winding banks of the Kyichu River. "Slow down, you crazy bastard," John called after we rounded a bend. I did not stop until I found a shutter that opened. When our eyes eventually adjusted to the darkness, we explored the Potala not open to the tourists.

We lost track of time, how many floors we hiked up or down, and where we were in the palace labyrinth. Lit matches cast eerie shadows on padlocked doors and clay hearths blanketed by dust. We tried to climb to the highest roof, but locked doors and dead ends forced us down into the Potala's depths. We negotiated stairwells clogged with broken timber, trash, and excrement, which left us silent for long periods. I thought of how easily the tourists had believed the tour guide and became angry at myself for not challenging her.

John wedged a copy of a U.S. Congressional resolution on human rights violations in Tibet, which he had gotten in New York prior to our departure, into a padlocked door. The resolution, dated June 7, 1987, stated succinctly that 1.2 million Tibetans had died from execution, imprisonment, and starvation in Tibet's thirty years of military occupation; that 6,254 monasteries had been destroyed, and only thirteen rebuilt; and that Tibet was being colonized by Han immigrants. "I had forgotten what a hard-hitting document this is," John said. He stopped to admire the piece of paper, which stood out like a flag from the door frame.

I asked John what he expected to accomplish by leaving the resolution, and how he thought the Chinese police would respond. John said that he had not thought about it. He disliked the fact that Tibetans got no information other than the Chinese party line from the *People's Daily*. I became angry at John in a way that I never had been before. As long as I had known him he had loved to indulge in these sorts of quixotic adventures; but leaving this resolution behind could get Tibetans in trouble. I started to yell at John for being reckless, but as usual his easy grin and humor disarmed me. We both realized that no one was likely to see the piece of paper for years, and we laughed at the idea of such an effete gesture.

Sunbeams straying into a corner of the dark hallway drew us to a room with a crack in its shutters that opened easily. I was surprised to see the late afternoon sun on Chokpori Hill, where Lhasa's most prestigious college of medicine once stood. The Fifth Dalai Lama had Chokpori Medical College built in the seventh century. Physicians from all over Mongolia and Tibet were educated there, until Chinese soldiers bombed it to the ground with artillery. Now all that remained was a television tower on a barren slope.

John leaned out the window and looked down two stories to a sloping ramp of trees. The cracks in the ancient mortar looked as though they could provide finger-width holds to the ramp. "We can downclimb this!" John exclaimed. As we made our way down the wall he talked about sharing the resolution with fellow travelers. He suggested that we leave the shutters unlocked; we could come back another night with other travelers and have a Potala party.

"We have to *do* something," John said.

I agreed with John that something had to be done about Tibet's plight. But I still needed to recuperate from Everest. I coveted my breakfasts of yogurt and fried eggs wrapped in pancakes with chocolate sauce at a Chinese restaurant. My afternoons were devoted to drinking cold beer in the hot sun and writing exaggerated postcards home at the Lhasa Cafe, a new restaurant in the Barkhor, where an Austrian chef made apple strudel, bratwurst, and potato salad. In the evenings I wanted to enjoy six-hour dinners with other travelers.

• • •

"How's the intrepid traveler?" John inquired as I sprinted out of bed and down the hall to the hotel's communal toilet. This particular toilet was a noisome reminder of other hygienic atrocities I'd experienced around the world. I held my breath.

Dysentery was not new to my travels. I had my first bout in 1979, mountaineering in Peru with John. After eating salad on our descent into the lowlands, I became stricken with diarrhea. Then, in 1983, after a month of not getting sick on rancid yak butter tea in Ladakh, in northern India, I considered myself immune; in the capital, Leh, I thought I could drink the water with impunity. One should never think one can drink or eat anything in Leh with impunity.

Squatting and holding my breath like this at 12,000 feet made me lightheaded. I envied John's intestinal fortitude. He ate ravenously and rarely had to run for a toilet, as I often did. John made fun of how I hoarded bits of newspaper, the small Tibetan currency notes worth two cents, even bus tickets. No scrap was too small, no parchment too rough that it could not be used in an emergency. I had eaten nonstop for two weeks and was still unable to gain weight, which made me wonder what sort of parasites I was hosting.

• • •

We met another American woman in the market. Julie had saved enough money working as a nursery-school teacher in Colorado to travel for six months in Asia. She traveled with a "male friend" from India to Pakistan, crossed the Karakoram Highway to Kashgar, and continued along the old silk road to Urumchi and Turfan before they split up. He went to Beijing. She came to Tibet. Both John and I told her we were glad she came to Tibet. Julie smiled. She planned to stay in Lhasa for a few weeks, then hitchhike to Everest. She also asked if we wanted to play hackysack in the Barkhor Square. We became an attraction among the chanting monks and Khampa dancers. John and I tried to outdo each other, intent on impressing Julie.

A Tibetan woman lunged for the Tibetan National Flag sticker on John's camera bag. "Watch it!" John warned. The woman lunged again for the sticker and berated John in Tibetan. I could not understand everything the woman said, but I recognized her hand in the shape of a pistol pointing to the sticker and back to John.

That night we ate dinner at Julie's favorite restaurant, the Sunflower Cafe, which was run by a cantankerous Chinese man who thought Tibet should be free. Lu served warm beer and charged too much for his mediocre food, which had to be eaten while sitting on miniature stools around miniature tables. But the atmosphere was appealing, and we became regulars.

One night Lu closed the restaurant after the other customers had left. We were drinking warm beer and blasting Dylan on Lu's tape deck, and John was talking about politics. We thought Lu was getting ready to push the six small tables together and get his bedding out from the kitchen, but instead he handed everyone at our table another can of beer, and said gruffly, "On the house for my American friends."

"You won't make any money if you give away beer," John said.

"Americans are good business!" Lu said. He smiled his rotten-teeth smile, then scrunched up his face. "There was a public execution in Lhasa today. Two Tibetans killed at the People's Stadium."

"Did you see it?" John asked.

"Had to. A representative from every business is required to go, then report back to others. China has executions every year before the People's Congress. This year, 15,000 people come." Everyone at the table strained to discern Lu's thick Chinese accent over the blaring tape deck. "The police tie prisoner's wrists behind back. After prisoner's crimes are announced, police pull up on wrists to break elbows. Then each prisoner is shot with one bullet in back of head. They charge family five dollars for bullet."

"That's on a par with the Khmer Rouge," Julie said. John and I agreed.

"Used to be worse," Lu said. "Before, they cut prisoner's tongue out. Otherwise Tibetans screamed, 'Free Tibet,' before they shot." Lu leaned forward to ask, "Why do my American friends think execution at this time?" Lu looked inquisitively at us, sitting in stunned silence. "Dalai Lama in United States now," Lu said. "He make political speech to U.S. Congress. China wants to show the world they will not be push around by U.S. government."

"How do you know this?" John asked.

"The Chinese broadcast it on the street," Lu said.

Two nights later Lu said there was a rainbow over Potala; that same night, all of us felt three subtle seismic tremors. "I am not religious," Lu said. "But I believe everyone should be free to practice religious. Rainbows and earthquakes are auspicious signs for Tibetans."

● ● ●

At 9:00 the next morning, September 27, 1987, one dozen monks from the Sera Monastery carrying homemade Tibetan flags began a circuit of the Jokhang Temple. The monks chanted, "Free Tibet," and "China out of Tibet." All business activity ceased as Tibetans left their shops and homes to march with the monks. By the third circuit there were 300 people marching and chanting. A dozen police arrived in jeeps and beat the monks with rifle butts, but they were vastly outnumbered, and the demonstrators continued toward the Cultural Palace.

A hundred yards ahead I saw a flash of maroon and yellow robes surrounded by men in green uniforms with raised truncheons. John, Julie, and I ran with Chinese, Tibetans, and tourists alike down the wide boulevard. On the sidewalk to our left, two policemen beat a Tibetan woman to the ground with their truncheons. Hundreds of people had stopped to watch but did nothing. I could not believe what I was seeing. I was also unable to intervene, and in the mayhem I briefly lost sight of

John. Julie and I ran toward the police jeeps that blocked the main intersection in front of the Cultural Palace.

Five young cadets stood at attention while a group of older police beat a Tibetan couple. The audible *crack* of a truncheon slicing a hunk of flesh from the man's head registered as terror on two of the young cadets' faces. Another cadet winced as the man fell to the ground. The cadets laughed nervously as their elders beat the woman on the head, back, and legs. A pair of policemen grabbed the man's wrists and ankles and swung his limp body onto the back of an open truck. The police continued to beat the woman as she climbed onto the truck to stay with the man.

Hundreds of people saw the Chinese police beat the Tibetans. No one tried to stop them. I counted eight monks thrown into the truck before it drove off. With the monks gone, the police raised their truncheons and dispersed the crowd still converging in front of the Cultural Palace. Suddenly, the three of us were holding hands and running down the wide boulevard away from the police.

CHAPTER SIX

ARREST

"JOHN'S BEEN ARRESTED," Julie said, when she found me eating *thukpa* (noodle soup) at a Tibetan restaurant the next day. "Two policemen saw John's sticker of the Tibetan flag. They interrogated us for hours. John got the police to let me go. You have to get all of your books out of your room—"

"*John's* books," I corrected her. The Tibetan woman in the market had warned John to take that damn sticker off, but he kept it, insistent on making a point—on not being intimidated. Julie immediately got up to leave. "Where are you going?" I asked.

"To clean my room before the police do. You'd better, too."

I thought of racing back to the room to retrieve John's books and my journal. Sitting there, I envisioned the police catching me when I tried to leave the room with the incendiary publications. I decided to finish my *thukpa* and then walk slowly back to the hotel. When I arrived, five policemen were already crammed into our tiny cubicle. John was with them.

"We have some trouble with your friend," a Chinese police captain said in English. "Wait outside." John looked with forlorn eyes at the books, papers, our passports, and my journal on the night table. Two Tibetan men in plainclothes sat next to John on his bed. One man was balding and had a paunch. The other was a teenager trying to grow sideburns. Two Chinese policemen in uniform sat on my bed. Our possessions lay strewn about the room. "Wait outside!" the captain said again.

I did not have to be told a third time. To my surprise no one followed. Long, panicky strides took me down the stairs to my bicycle and the street. If the police found John's resolutions where they were hidden in the ceiling, he could go to prison. I did not think the police would physically hurt him, but he could be learning Chinese the hard way for an indefinite period of time. I was sure I too would be arrested once they read my journal. Although I had liked the individual Chinese people we had met, every page of my journal mourned some aspect of China's occupation and colonization of Tibet. I resolved to eat as much as I could while I remained free.

•   •   •

A stiff hand on my shoulder interrupted my second steaming bowl of *thukpa*. "We got the stickers in Hong Kong," John whispered quickly. "They don't know about the resolution yet."

"I told you to take that damned sticker off," I whispered back, before seeing the two Chinese policemen behind John. "*Ni hao,*" I greeted the first man in Chinese. He led me out of the restaurant and prevented John from getting into the jeep that had brought them. I dropped my bicycle key out the window for John before the police and I sped off through the cobblestone streets.

The jeep's screeching siren warned the pedestrians and bicyclists, who fled from its path. I felt a visceral sense of helplessness that reminded me of when I had been arrested twice, in New York City, when I worked on the United Farm Workers grape boycott in 1976. Still an idealistic teenager, I had been arrested for posting colorful "BOYCOTT SCAB GRAPES AND LETTUCE" stickers in the subway, then a week later for singing, "We Shall Overcome" in a supermarket that sold scab grapes. Both times a judge heard my case and released me within twenty-four hours.

A Chinese woman selling preserved apricots outside the Banak Shol hotel jumped as the jeep skidded to a halt inches from her stand. A Swedish couple registering at the desk paused to watch us. I had no thought of fleeing as the police led me up the stairs.

"You will call me Mr. Chen," the police captain said, standing at attention. He had a hard face and eyes that gave nothing away. He picked up my journal with its sticker of the Tibetan national flag and said, "First we have trouble with your friend. Now we have trouble with you. Where did you get this flag?"

"It's not a flag," I said. "It's a sticker."

"It is Tibetan flag!" Mr. Chen screamed. "Tibet is part of China!"

Even if the five policemen and I had been friends we would have been uncomfortable in such a cramped space. I opened a pack of Marlboros and offered one to Mr. Chen. He refused automatically, refused a second time, then finally accepted a cigarette. So did the Chinese deputies and the undercover Tibetans.

"You don't smoke?" Mr. Chen asked.

"It's bad for your health," I said.

Mr. Chen proceeded to attack me with a barrage of questions: Where did I get the flag? How many did I bring into Tibet? Who did I give them to? Where? Why? I tried to answer each question correctly. None of the police seemed to mind when John walked in and sat down next to me. After an hour, Mr. Chen grabbed my journal and our passports. The deputies took the stack of evidence. "You are forbidden to leave your room tonight," Mr. Chen said. "You will report to the police station tomorrow morning at ten."

After they left, John said, "The young Tibetan trying to grow sideburns and the Chinese mute took Julie and me off the street at gunpoint. I had a resolution in my camera bag. They took us to the police station and interrogated us for three hours. The deputies kept looking at the Tibetan flag. They inspected it, fondled it. In a way I think they were fascinated by it. I was terrified they were going to open the bag and see the resolution."

A grin broke across John's face. "It didn't take long to figure out how to try to get rid of the resolution. I stood up and grabbed the bag. They were as surprised as I was. Then I pretended that I had explosive diarrhea. One of the policemen led me to their bathroom. He tried to watch me go. 'No way!' I shouted, and slammed the door shut. Then I dropped our resolution into the black hole."

The siren from the departing police jeep drove us to the window. The two deputies had been stationed as guards at the hotel's front door.

"Thanks for getting me arrested," I said.

"We wouldn't be if you had cleaned the room before the police came. Didn't Julie tell you?" he replied. For a second John became livid with anger, then said, "What does Chen mean by having us return to the police station at ten? Let's find Julie and get some beer," John said.

"What about the deputies?"

"You must be flustered," John chided. "If the chance to see Julie doesn't make you want to sneak out of here now, think what miserable company you'll make in prison."

Even when I was mad at John, I couldn't stay mad at him for long. John's good humor had enabled me to rappel twenty pitches in a blizzard off El Capitan, to almost enjoy shivering all night in a boxcar going east when we wanted to be going west, and to tease that Julie wanted me, not him.

That night I could feel myself losing the ability to distinguish fantasy from reality, paranoia from fear. I lay awake worrying that the police would read my journal and discover that I despised the Chinese occupation of Tibet. What I had seen in Tibet affected me deeply. The Tibetans were tourist attractions in their own country, the way native Americans are in parts of the United States.

The next morning, John assembled paper, pen, money, cigarettes, and condoms on his bed in preparation for our trip to the police station. For John, going to jail was another adventure, like hopping trains or climbing Everest. I asked if he thought we were going to summer camp. John didn't take the bait. Looking out the window and seeing that there were no guards and no jeep to drive us to the police station, he said, "If they won't drive us, I'm going to take my time getting there." I put water purification tablets in my left sock, antibiotics in the right.

We pedaled slowly through the park behind the Potala toward the station. The smell of rotting leaves made me homesick for New England's fall explosion of color—anywhere but this windswept desert. Then John stopped his bicycle next to a beautiful Tibetan girl and motioned for her to get on. She hopped sidesaddle across the back of the bicycle and wrapped her arms around his waist. Her long black hair swayed as John wobbled to a start. Soon the three of us were laughing as we wound our way through the park.

• • •

Under different circumstances the Tibetan rugs and couches that decorated the station might have lent it a pleasant air. Mr. Chen stood up from his desk. His face looked stern. "Sit down," he ordered, pointing to the couch near his desk. "You will begin by telling me your professions, and where you live."

"We are students," I said.

"You are not student!" Mr. Chen shouted. "Mr. Ackerly. Where are you from?"

"Washington, D.C." John said.

"Washington!" Mr. Chen yelled. "Home of CIA! What is CIA doing in China?"

"We are tourists," John protested.

Mr. Chen slapped the table and screamed. "Tibet is part of China! You are not tourists! You work for CIA. You come to China to make trouble." The jugular veins on Mr. Chen's neck bulged as he repeated the same questions that we had already answered. John maintained that we had gotten the flags from a street vendor in Hong Kong, and that neither of us could remember what the man looked like or where his shop was. In spite of Mr. Chen's yelling, John remained pleasant and calm. He also tried to appease Mr. Chen.

"What does 'national' mean?" Mr. Chen yelled, holding John's camera bag with the sticker of the Tibetan national flag inches from John's face.

"We have the same thing in our country," John said. "Each state has its own flag. It represents its own distinct area, the way Tibet is a distinct part of China."

"National means independent. Tibet is not independent. What does 'national' mean?"

"In the United States," I said, hoping to distract Mr. Chen, "native American Indians used to live all across the country before the Europeans came. Now there are relatively few Indians left."

"Yes!" Mr. Chen exclaimed. "What would you say if your Indians cried, 'Free America?'"

"They still cry, 'Free America,'" I said.

"Tibet is part of China."

"Just since your military invaded—" I interrupted. John kicked me under the table.

"Tibet has never been independent," Mr. Chen screamed. "Tibet will never be independent. Tibet is part of China." Mr. Chen did not hit me, but I think the thought crossed his mind. Instead of yelling at me again, he said, "In China, we have ways of changing your attitude." He walked to a back room to yell first at his deputies and then into a phone.

"Do you *want* to get your passport back?" John hissed. "I forgot to tell you—they found the picture of us with that Reagan cut-out."

"No wonder they think we're CIA."

"They thought Reagan was for real," John said. "I didn't say anything. I wasn't sure if it would help us or hurt us." After a long silence, John said, "China doesn't put U.S. citizens in prison."

"They will if they read my journal."

John laughed. "I'd be worried too if I had written what you did. So *don't* argue with Chen," he whispered, as Mr. Chen emerged from the back room.

"China signed the Geneva convention in 1981 regarding the acceptable treatment of prisoners," John announced. "I would like to see the statutes that we have violated. In English. It's international law."

Mr. Chen pointed to a poster behind his desk that I had been too scared to notice. "'Article Five,'" Mr. Chen said. "'Aliens are forbidden by Chinese law to endanger the national security interests of China, harm its public interests, or disturb its public order.'"

"How have we endangered China's national security interests?" John asked.

Mr. Chen slammed his fist on the table. For a second I thought I might get to kick John. John's face turned the same shade of red as Mr. Chen's, but he managed to suppress his anger.

Our interrogations took on a regular pattern. Mr. Chen repeated the same series of questions. John tried to placate Mr. Chen and kicked me under the table when I argued. I began to sense that underneath Mr. Chen's hard police exterior, he himself was seeking answers to the questions that he asked. John's training as a lawyer gave him remarkable grace under the pressure of interrogation. Before law school, John had been defenseless when anyone yelled at him. As for me, I was a victim of passion and mood, which had just been made worse by medical school.

A group of French trekkers came into the station to get Alien Travel

Permits. Mr. Chen retreated into the back room while one of the deputies issued the permits. John produced a deck of cards and played solitaire. I became so curious about the back room that I meandered over to the slightly open door. Mr. Chen stood over the Tibetan trying to grow sideburns; both men were intent on my journal. Seeing this— even more than John kicking me under the table—prompted me to stop arguing with Mr. Chen.

"The Dalai Lama say many things to your government," Mr. Chen said when he returned. "China get bad press. We don't know what we're going to do with you. But we're going to punish you." Mr. Chen let the seriousness of our situation register on our faces before he continued, "Report here tomorrow morning at 10:00. You must write self-criticisms and bring them with you."

After being interrogated for eight hours, John and I were allowed to ride our bicycles back to our hotel without a police escort. We should have been elated, but we continued to argue. I said we should consider trying to leave Lhasa immediately. John said he wasn't going anywhere until he got his passport back.

● ● ●

"How's this for a self-criticism?" John said, reading from a page in his journal later that night. "'I apologize for any trouble I may have caused the People's Republic of China. I have always been an admirer of the People's Revolution, and supported the People's Republic of China. It was not my intent to harm anyone by bringing postcards of the Dalai Lama to Tibetans. I am sorry for the trouble that this careless deed has caused me, and for the shame it has cast upon my ancestors.'" John looked up with glee. "They'll love the line about bringing shame to my ancestors," he said. "The Chinese really relate to that kind of stuff. What did you write?"

"Nothing."

"But Mr. Chen—"

I interrupted John by asking if he still had his map of the Dalai Lama's escape route in 1959. "Now you're talking like the old Blake," he said. John retrieved the folded paper from his pack and surveyed the route from Lhasa across the Himalayas to Bhutan. "It took the Dalai

Lama several weeks to cross the Himalayas," John said. "It's a direct route. If we're considering an overland escape, I think we should cross into Nepal near Everest, where we already know the route. It's almost October: if there's a storm, if we choose the wrong pass, we could freeze to death. We'll have to avoid being seen the whole time. The border will be intense. We could say that we lost everything in an avalanche."

This John, the one I knew and loved, disappeared again after only a moment, replaced by the poised lawyer. He refolded the map. "The more I think about sneaking out of Tibet," John said, "the more it makes sense to stay. Mr. Chen will return our passports tomorrow. He has to. China has to officially notify any foreign national's government within forty-eight hours of his arrest."

* * *

"Our superiors in Beijing have decided to release you," Mr. Chen announced at four the next afternoon, after we had spent six hours that day in the station. "You will pay $200 each for a flight to Beijing tomorrow."

"We don't have enough money for a flight anywhere," John lied.

Mr. Chen disappeared yet again into the back room. I knew that John was pushing him, testing the limits. This time it worked. Mr. Chen returned our passports and John's camera bag and said that we had four days to leave by bus. John argued that we should have at least ten days, and got the extra time. My journal was brought out next. It had a clean rectangular patch in the center where the sticker had been torn off. The police, it appeared, had not been able to decipher my handwriting. Mr. Chen sat next to John and opened my journal to the last page.

"What is this?" Mr. Chen yelled, his voice sounding enraged.

"It's nothing," John said, easing my journal from Mr. Chen's hands and dropping it into my lap. "It's just about the demonstration. Everyone's talking about it. It's no secret."

I said that I had only written about the demonstration on the last page. Noticing Julie's name in the paragraph before the demonstration, I pointed this out and said, "This is about, you know . . . sex." Mr. Chen blushed when I moved my index finger in and out of my fist. He approved when I tore the offending pages out, and struggled to maintain his composure while I shredded the pages into the ash tray. Soon after John and I were racing our bicycles down the street, away from the station.

• • •

Lu let us cook dinner in his kitchen that night. Julie and I chopped garlic and ginger while John stirred the wok. Otto supervised. We played rock and roll too loud on Lu's rickety tape deck as I put eleven cloves of garlic into the stir fry and Julie poured in a healthy splash of warm beer. My arm tingled expectantly when it touched hers as we worked side by side in the kitchen. Earlier, as we had walked to Lu's place from the hotel, Julie and I had first discussed the prospect of spending the night together.

"Tomorrow is Chinese National Day," John said to no one in particular.

"Like Fourth of July in America?" Otto said. "Lots of boom-boom. Tomorrow I make my own boom-boom. Today I bought a Chinese flag to burn."

"They'll shoot you," John said.

"Is no problem," Otto said and waved his hand. "In Germany, I burn already ten, eleven American flags at demonstrations. Tomorrow I burn one Chinese flag. No problem."

Lu stormed into the kitchen. He looked disgruntled. "I had trouble with police," Lu said. "Three come in earlier. They want to eat free. I let them eat, but not for free."

"Won't that cause trouble for you later?" Julie asked.

"Everything cause trouble for me later," Lu said.

CHAPTER SEVEN

CHINESE NATIONAL DAY

O N OCTOBER 1, Chinese National Day, no one had any idea that Lhasa would erupt in the largest nationalist uprisings witnessed by Westerners since the Chinese invasion of Tibet in 1950. As they had four days before, a handful of Buddhist monks circumambulated the Jokhang Temple at 9:00 that morning. The monks carried outlawed Tibetan flags and chanted, "China out of Tibet." Pilgrims stopped prostrating. Urchins stopped tugging on tourists' sleeves. Monks stopped chanting scripture. Women stopped hawking necklaces of cheap turquoise. All business activity ceased as Tibetans left their shops and homes to follow the monks.

At the completion of their third circuit around the Jokhang, hundreds of chanting Tibetans faced seven jeep-loads of police. The police beat the demonstrators with shovels and rifle butts. In the time it took the police to drag twenty monks into a nearby police station, the crowd outside swelled to about a thousand. Gunfire inside the building apparently made the crowd of Tibetans believe that the police were killing the monks.

I learned all of this from Julie, when she returned to find me breakfasting on sweet tea and yogurt on the third-floor balcony of our hotel. Julie had gotten up and gone out early, and had seen the crowd grow so fast that she knew something horrible was going to happen. By the time she returned I had already seen the column of black smoke rising above the Tibetan rooftops in the distance. John had come by fifteen minutes earlier to tell me he was going out on his bicycle, convinced that something important was going on. He had kept us up late the night before talking in legalese about how China's "liberation" of Tibet was a euphemism for colonialism and violated international law. Now it seemed that Tibet's unrest under Chinese domination might be erupting into violence. The thought of treating wounded demonstrators terrified me. As a newly minted physician I had never treated patients on my own. I stuffed bandages and antibiotics into my shoulder bag.

Julie and I held hands as we ran among the hundreds of people flocking to the Barkhor Square. The streets were so crowded that people had climbed on top of the metal fence around the Tibetan Medical Institute to look into the square. I searched the crowd for John; he was probably in front of the Jokhang. A police line kept us from crossing the open square, where a single overturned police jeep poured smoke into the air. A soldier raised his AK-47 to strike a Tibetan woman who tried to step through the line.

"Should we go back to our hotel?" a couple obviously from the Lhasa Hotel asked us from where they stood at a bus stop. "Isn't this exciting! What's happening?"

A shrill cry came from a Chinese man twenty feet away who was being beaten by a crowd of Tibetans. Blood spurted from his head amid a swarm of fists. He cried for mercy as the Tibetans beat him with stones and stripped the film from his camera. I felt a wave of revulsion for the Tibetans. No one deserves to be beaten. Desperately flailing his arms, the man broke free and ran toward a group of Chinese watching from a distance.

A troupe of "*kuchi kuchi*" children chased another Chinese man who was trying to ride his bicycle through the mayhem. The children threw rocks that thumped against his back. One rock hit the man's head and sent his bicycle reeling. The children shrieked and threw more rocks. They treated the Chinese man the way they might have tortured an insect.

The crowd parted for a fire truck that I assumed would be used to extinguish the burning jeep. Instead, soldiers on top of the truck aimed the hose into the crowd. Sixty soldiers goose-stepped toward the crowd from behind the truck. The sound of coordinated boot steps striking the cobblestones punctuated the soldiers' collective yell. Instead of stopping to extinguish the burning jeep, the fire truck headed toward the Jokhang.

Defiant fists rose out of the crowd of Tibetans guarding their most holy temple. They threw a volley of rocks that shattered the fire truck's windshield. The truck made a U-turn and the soldiers followed. The Tibetans cheered. Julie and I took the opportunity to sneak past a policeman who had turned to watch the fracas. We sprinted in a wide arc around the burning jeep, wider around the truck and retreating police, and joined the thousand-strong crowd of Tibetans who were cheering and crying in front of the Jokhang.

Tibetan women alongside the monastery's outer wall were pounding the street's cobblestones into baseball-sized pieces, which the children in the crowd scattered at everyone's feet. A monk standing on the Jokhang's roof raised his fists and yelled down into the square. The woman next to me screamed, "They're killing our monks." I looked around for John and saw another crowd forming in front of the police station. More overturned vehicles clogged the alley.

The Tibetans next to me stoned a Tibetan man who had been taking photographs of the crowd. The man dropped his camera and fought for his life. The Tibetans are killing their own people, I thought; had they gone mad? Suddenly it dawned on me that this Tibetan must be an undercover policeman, like the other man with a camera. Their developed film would have been used to identify and arrest people later.

Julie was gone. I called her name and looked frantically around the crowd. I needed to find her, John, a familiar face. A crackling sound stampeded the crowd. I found myself stooped over, scurrying toward the burning vehicles. I ran past an overturned jeep with a young boy squatting next to a puddle of leaking gas. I spotted a policemen on the roof and jumped into an alcove where several families had taken refuge. Most of the people looked frightened. Two of the Tibetan men in the alcove stepped out into the alley, threw rocks at the policeman on the roof, and ducked back.

The two men laughed. They seemed deranged, and they presented easy targets for the police. A withered Tibetan woman with a baby in her lap motioned for me to come farther inside as the men stepped into the alley to throw another rock. When they returned to the alcove amid a burst of firecrackers, their faces were frozen in terror.

I peered around the corner and saw a woman shouting at the head of a crowd in front of the police station. Five Khampas with red tassels

wrapped around their heads ran up to the station and climbed in
through the broken first-floor windows. Other men followed. Soon
every window had Tibetans climbing into them. Office furniture and
police files were thrown out of the windows and piled at the station's
front door. Boys lit the pile using gasoline-soaked rags. The flames
quickly engulfed the mountain of furniture and paper and reached up to
the police on the roof. A nearby explosion paralyzed me, and I felt my
heart thundering in my chest. A tire had exploded on one of the vehicles; I felt my arms and legs to make sure they were all there.

More fireworks from the rooftop drove home the sickening realization that the sounds I was hearing were actually weapons fire. I thought
for a second about how easily human flesh is torn, took a deep breath,
and ran out of the alcove and back to the Jokhang. I found Julie holding
a Tibetan woman's hand in front of the two-story pillars at the
Jokhang's main entrance. The three of us embraced. Tears rolled off the
woman's ruddy cheeks. She said something that neither Julie nor I
understood and we started crying. I cried for the Tibetan children
throwing rocks at the Chinese and for what it must have been like to
grow up in Lhasa. I also cried for the Tibetans still inside the police station, and for John, who I hoped was not hurt, or worse. But mostly I
cried for the fear of losing my life.

"John's taking pictures in front of the police station," Julie said. "I'm
running film for him. It's a miracle Otto hasn't been shot. He's at the
front of the crowd, throwing rocks at the soldiers."

* * *

Four running men carrying a monk on their shoulders materialized out
of the smoke. The men ran as fast as they could and seemed to transport
the monk effortlessly. Bullets strafed the wall over the men's heads.
They ducked and kept running toward us. Even at a distance, I could
see the monk was badly burned. A policeman on the roof took a bead on
the men with his pistol as they ran. Everyone around me was crying.

"*Amchi yin*" (doctor am), I said, and the crowd let me squeeze closer
to the monk. He appeared to be unconscious. The skin on his arms,
face, neck, and head was covered with second- and third-degree burns.
Large sheets of flesh hung from his scarlet arms like onion skin. I could

see in an instant that he needed intravenous fluids, antibiotics, and sterile bandages, none of which were available. Instead, the crowd lifted the monk overhead. He opened his eyes and raised a clenched fist. Everyone cheered.

The sweet smell of the monk's cooked flesh made me gag. I could do nothing for him except document what I had seen. The crowd headed toward the soldiers at the far side of the square. The soldiers fidgeted with their machine guns. They looked nervous, as though they did not know how to respond to the angry Tibetans.

A Tibetan man came toward me carrying a small boy in his arms. Blood poured from the boy's mouth and soaked the left side of his shirt. The man stared straight ahead. The boy looked up at me with weak eyes as I examined where the bullet had entered through a small hole near his heart and exited through his back. The boy needed a trauma surgery team. I pressed my hand onto the wounds as life faded from his eyes. His dazed father kept carrying the boy through the maddening crowd. There was nothing I could do. I looked for a weed or tuft of grass with which to wipe the blood from my hands.

Six men carried another man on a table through fifty yards of machine-gun fire on the ground in front of the police station, dodging single rounds from snipers on the roof. Even before they arrived I could see that the man on the table was dead. Pink foam oozed from his nose and mouth. His neck was warm but he had no pulse. Like the boy, he had been shot through the chest from the front, but this bullet had gone through his heart.

Eight small children hiding behind an overturned jeep used slings to throw rocks at the police in front of the burning station. They used the same slings that the shepherd boys had shown us in the mountains, but they were not old enough to make them *CRACK* when the rock shot out. The police fired back over the children's heads. I doubted the kids understood that they could be killed by the police. "Stop," I yelled at the children, but they didn't listen.

A group of Tibetans huddled in the middle of the square. My first "*Amchi yin*" got me close enough to see a woman in a lavender *chuba* cradling the head of a sixteen-year-old boy. The bone structure and soft tissue on the right side of the boy's face had been completely caved in by multiple blows with a blunt object. A Tibetan man wearing a business suit told me in broken English that the police had beat the boy inside the station. I watched the woman pour water from a chalice into her son's unresponsive mouth. The boy was dead.

A war cry rose from a line of soldiers at the far end of the square. Their cry continued as they ran toward the Jokhang. Tibetans in front of the temple raised their fists in the air. The thought of fleeing did not occur to me. I picked up rocks along with the hundreds of Tibetans all around me. In a desperate reaction to the killing I became part of the violence myself. "Motherfuckers," I yelled at the oncoming soldiers. "Die, motherfuckers," I screamed with the first volley of rocks.

To my amazement, the soldiers turned in mid-stride and fled before our mob. We chased the soldiers off the end of the square and down the wide boulevard toward the Cultural Palace. This ignited cheers from the Tibetans, as though for a day they had reclaimed Lhasa.

* * *

At dusk I stared at the smoldering remains of the collapsed police station. I still had not found John or Julie. Besides the few Tibetans who were sifting china cups and other such prizes from the rubble, I was surprised to see how quickly the pilgrims had resumed their circumambulations of the Jokhang. Amazingly, tourists were browsing among the stalls, most of which had already been set up again. A young man I had never seen before approached me and asked, "Are you the American doctor?" in an English accent. He introduced himself as Andrew and asked if I would come with him to treat a man he knew of who had been shot in the ankle. During the riot Andrew had put a pressure dressing on the wound, and had gotten directions to the man's home.

Between the two of us we confirmed six deaths that we had witnessed personally: two monks in their twenties shot with AK-47s; one ten-year-old boy shot through the chest; a thirty-six-year-old woman shot in the head; a thirty-five-year old man shot in the heart; and a sixteen-year-old boy beaten to death inside the police station. Andrew recorded each detail in a notebook.

Snapping his head from side to side as though he were still under fire, Andrew led me along the shadows from the two- and three-story Tibetan buildings, where darkness hid the dirt but not the smell of the excrement spread onto the streets. I walked quickly behind him, carrying a rock in each hand. After throwing rocks at the police I was nervous about carrying them now, but I was afraid of being attacked by mongrels. Lhasa's dogs were out in force.

Headlights swept toward us across the cobblestones and we ducked into a side alley. A Lhasa Apso barked ferociously, and just got louder after I pretended to throw a rock at it. The dog continued to bark while a Toyota Land Cruiser filled with Chinese police drove slowly past the alley. We crossed a well-lit area that cast an eerie glow over a pack of mongrels heaped in confusion against a wall. Piled on top of each other they looked like adorable children; I counted fourteen of them before we rounded the corner.

"This is it," Andrew said in front of a large wooden door. He knocked using its serpentine brass ring and shouted in Tibetan that he was with a Western doctor. Two men appeared in the alley and I turned to the wall and pretended to urinate. Andrew continued to knock and yell—too loudly, I thought. I became convinced that the whole neighborhood could hear him. He didn't even know for certain if this was the man's house.

Footsteps approached from inside. Andrew started speaking in Tibetan, then in Chinese. "Shit," he said, walking away. "When I was talking in Tibetan, she said this was the right house. But my Chinese is better than my Tibetan. Once I switched she said that the man had already gone to the hospital."

Andrew said that he knew of another man who had been shot in the leg. "He's somewhere near here," he said. After we first knocked loudly at two wrong doors, a woman let us into her home.

"Thank you for coming," the woman whispered before closing the wooden shutters. "I know how dangerous the streets are after dark." She wore a colorful striped apron over a turquoise *chuba*. "My name is Pema. I am sorry that we have to be so secretive." Pema smiled as she said this and I noticed that she spoke fluent British-accented English. In the dim light she motioned for us not to make a sound. We followed her up wooden stairs that were so steep I had to use the handrail.

"There are informers in every compound," Pema whispered. "One of the neighbors will report us if they see us coming in or out." The darkness scared me, but I was more afraid of not being able to help anyone who had been shot in the leg.

"I'm pleased to meet you," Pema's brother said, lifting a heavy hand to greet us. He said his name was Tsering. They were Nepalese Tibetans who had come to visit relatives in Lhasa. Tsering pulled the sheet back to reveal dirty, blood-soaked gauze wrapped too tightly around his right thigh. Most of the blood on the bandage had dried. Both of his feet had good pulses and color, which meant that the bullet had not severed an artery. I asked Tsering if he could move his toes, which he did, slowly. He could also move his foot and raise his leg.

Andrew asked a series of questions to find out what Tsering had seen. A Tibetan doctor had stitched Tsering up and discharged him before the police surrounded the *Mendzekhang*. Tsering went on to say that he had heard of wounded Tibetans who went to the People's Hospital, the only place where Tibetans had access to Western medicine, and the doctors there sent them to prison.

Tsering looked more relaxed than I felt. I couldn't remove bullets without hemostats or injectable anesthetic; I had only bandages and antibiotics. Butter lamps beneath an eight-by-ten-inch color photo of the Dalai Lama lent an air of calm to the room. Pema poured cups of butter tea and my stomach shuddered. I sipped the tea anyway and found it to have a fresh, clean taste. I thanked Pema in Tibetan and she refilled the cup to the brim after the first sip.

"You speak Tibetan well," Pema said.

I smiled back. Tibetans always said this no matter how little Tibetan you spoke. I asked if she had any boiling water with which to wash my hands.

Pema shook her head yes from side to side the way Indian and Nepalese people do. "I am familiar enough with Western medicine to know that you would need lots of boiling water."

Pema poured hot water over my hands and the dried blood coming off my fingers unleashed mental images of the riot: the burned monk, the boy beaten to death inside the police station, the man shot in the heart. Tears blurred my vision for an instant. Pema offered me a filthy towel, but I air-dried my hands instead.

"Did the bullet go in here?" Andrew asked as I dabbed gauze on the bloody, fingertip-sized holes in Tsering's thigh.

Tsering beamed. "In one side. Out the other."

"Where were you when you were shot?" Andrew asked.

"I was standing in the alley next to the police station," Tsering said. "The police were shooting pistols and machine guns from the rooftops and the street. I was looking right up at the policeman on the roof who was aiming down at me with his machine gun. A monk next to me was hit first. Then something hot ripped through my leg and I knew I was hit."

"What happened to the monk?" Andrew asked.

Tsering turned his head to stare straight up at the ceiling. A single tear rolled down his unshaven cheek. "The bullet blew the back of his head off. Blood got in my eyes. I couldn't see anything after that. Someone dragged me back."

I cleaned the entrance and exit wounds with hydrogen peroxide, imagining the tunnel of macerated flesh through the thickest part of Tsering's thigh. He needed intravenous antibiotics in a hospital. If an infection set in he could die, or at least need to have his leg amputated. By adding a mere squeeze of antibacterial cream, I was just putting a Band-Aid on an abyss. After rewrapping Tsering's thigh with a clean roll of gauze, I asked if his leg hurt.

"No," Tsering replied, and we both laughed. I knew he was lying. It was an odd moment to laugh but it made me feel better.

"You're a lucky man to have such a wonderful woman taking care of you," I said, and paused for their full attention before asking if Tsering had ever had a bad reaction to Western medicine before. I explained how to take the antibiotic pills and Tsering reached up and squeezed my hand. After effusive thanks and a few last sips of butter tea, Pema hurried us out into the dark hall. Before entering the street, Pema thanked us for saving her brother's life. I said that I would bring more antibiotics later.

"Please don't come back," Pema said. "It is too dangerous. If the police see you . . ."

"Wait," Andrew said, as I left to go off in search of John and Julie. "I need your help at a meeting."

CHAPTER EIGHT

LHASA BY NIGHT

ONE HUNDRED FOREIGNERS who had witnessed the riot had gathered in a dormitory room at one of the Tibetan hotels. I was so glad to see John and Julie sandwiched on a bed with eight other travelers that I didn't hear Andrew yelling from the middle of the room. John said he had spent the entire day in front of the police station. He photographed Tibetans besieging the police station and burning it to the ground; police taking pictures and video of the crowd from the rooftops; and police firing AK-47s and automatic pistols from the rooftops and the street. Julie had hidden three rolls of John's film.

"The telex and trunks have been down for three days," Andrew shouted. He held a clipboard as he spoke to the throng of people still buzzing with a cacophony of Asian and Indo-European languages. "There are no press here as yet. Which makes it imperative that we accurately record confirmed, first-hand accounts of what happened for the press when they do arrive. Before we start, I will state for the record that the purpose of this gathering is wholly nonviolent. As a group, we must condemn those individuals who threw rocks at the police."

"I throw rocks at Chinese police if I want," Otto shouted from a bunk bed in the back of the room. Other travelers who had participated in the demonstration hurled insults and profanity at Andrew. The meeting swiftly disintegrated into mayhem. I wanted to tell John and Julie what I had seen but I was mute. Even though I was a physician I felt unable to save anyone from dying. Throwing rocks at the police was the only thing I could do to try to stop the killing. Andrew gave up insisting that the rock throwers should be condemned and moved on to the next item on his list.

Andrew was a great organizer: he had to be in order to extract useful information out of the chaotic meeting. In less than an hour he confirmed that an additional six Tibetan men, women, monks, and children had died from gunshot wounds or beatings. "I'm afraid the police are taking the wounded to prison," Andrew said. "Now, an American doctor who treated a man who was shot has something to say."

Unexpectedly, I faced the crowd. I had always been afraid of speaking in public. I mentioned the wounded hiding in their homes who feared arrest if they went to the Chinese-run hospital. I estimated that there were ten times the number of wounded to the number of dead, and said that we needed more bandages and medicine. Julie volunteered to make the rounds of the Tibetan hotels later and collect medicine.

"The police are coming!" a voice outside the window called. People stampeded through the only door. I peered out the window and saw a Tibetan boy who worked at the hotel standing in the shadows. There were no police in sight, but I had no doubt that the meeting had been too loud.

• • •

Hours after the meeting, Julie and I fell asleep in each other's arms in her room. Lobsang, a Tibetan man who worked at the hotel, awoke us at six the next morning with homemade *momos* (yak meat dumplings) and tomato-egg soup. "Very good," Lobsang whispered excitedly to Julie. "Thank you for your help. Any wounded Tibetans, I am sending to you."

"No tourists with sore throats," I said.

"Yes," Lobsang said, smiling broadly. "Don't forget—I am not English-speaking. If the Chinese find out, I am finished." Lobsang excused his still-smiling self and we organized the assortment of medicine that Julie had collected into piles of antibiotics, pain medicine, antiseptics, and bandages. We had one pair of hemostats to use removing bullets, but no sterile gloves or injectable anesthetic. The different kinds of antibiotics we did have could provide broad-spectrum coverage for infections. This could save lives.

Andrew came in with a handsome blond couple. Heidi was a Swedish woman who, like me, had just graduated from medical school. She and I talked about not being able to do anything really helpful, and doing more harm than good if we were caught. Mark had a full beard and wore wool Tibetan pants and a vest. He looked like Saint Nicholas and turned out to be a lawyer from Australia who had lived in Tibet for the past eight months. He spoke good Tibetan and Mandarin. His dress and gentle demeanor stood out in marked contrast to Andrew, who wore a green army coat.

"You look tired," Julie said to Andrew.

"I was up all night," Andrew said, "trying to find someone at the Lhasa Hotel who would take a roll of film to Hong Kong. Let's get started, shall we?" Andrew opened his clipboard and said that he had met a Norwegian orthopedic surgeon who would act as a back-up if anything happened to Heidi or myself. The five of us would work as a team.

"This room will be our temporary base of operations," Andrew said. "Mark, you and Heidi comb the Barkhor for contacts to more wounded. Stick to people you can trust, like elders and monks. Blake and I will meet you at ten in front of the Jokhang. I met a monk yesterday who told me there were many wounded monks hiding inside the monastery. I set up a meeting. Julie, you stay here and coordinate incoming messages. We should all meet back here at noon."

* * *

At ten, when we all met at the main entrance to the Jokhang, a group of Chinese and Tibetan men were looking intently at two posters glued to the monastery walls. One poster was printed in Tibetan, the other in Chinese. I stepped closer to read them and two of the men raised their truncheons. I had to jump back to avoid being hit. Apparently, the men were police.

"Keep walking," Mark said. As we continued on he explained, "Those are posters from the underground. I saw them go up early in the morning before the undercover police staked them out. They say, 'Ten to twenty people died yesterday. Ten to twenty more may die. It does not matter. The Chinese have been here for thirty years. Now is the time to act.'"

By now, circumambulating the Jokhang had almost become second nature. Not only did I recognize individual vendors selling jewelry, but also monks who had stayed in the same place reciting scriptures for weeks. One pilgrim stood out more than the rest. Regardless of the time of day he was naked from the waist up and did prostrations around the Jokhang. At first his spasmodic movements and piercing stares had frightened me. Today he smiled, and I felt an unspoken kinship with him.

Convinced that a side door near the Jokhang's main entrance would open, Andrew stationed himself next to fifty older Tibetan men and women doing full-length prostrations. Like inchworms moving in place, they stretched out over the stones and then stood up, raising their clasped hands to the sky. Andrew devoted his undivided attention to the wooden door, which was obviously bolted on the outside. A small eddy of onlookers gathered in the stream. Even the Tibetans were wondering what he was doing. Andrew was a menace; I was sure he would get us all arrested. Heidi slipped a hand under Andrew's arm and gently coaxed him away.

Mark led the four of us past the prostrators into the temple's main entrance. Five somber Tibetan monks with well-muscled arms blocked the stairwell. Mark explained that Heidi and I were Western doctors and we were led up the steep stairs to the roof. Strings of prayer flags ran from the tips of the many-terraced roof to the tops of its golden spires, and carved wooden dragons jutted out from the corners like medieval gargoyles. We crossed several terraces, ran twice across open stretches, and climbed down some steep stairs to a dank room permeated by the smell of rancid yak butter and incense.

Our first patient told Mark that he had been shot in the stomach. He pulled up his shirt to reveal bloody gauze wrapped around his abdomen. Fortunately, the laceration skimmed but did not enter his side. "Kelsang was standing in front of the police station when a policeman on the roof shot him," Mark said. I had been so absorbed with Kelsang's wound that I had not heard him talking the whole time.

"How many demonstrations has Lhasa had?" Andrew asked.

"Since 1959," Mark translated, "there have been many major demonstrations that these monks know of, all as large as yesterday's riot. Yesterday was different only because Western travelers witnessed it."

A dozen pus-filled craters dotted the next monk's forehead. The oily salve he'd put on it made his burns look worse than they were. He held out a wide-mouth jar for us to examine the preparation of ground herbs it held. In my fledgling Tibetan I said, "Tibetan medicine is good." The monk nodded and stared deep into Heidi's beautiful cerulean eyes. Heidi told Mark to explain how important it was for the monk to avoid touching his face, and to wash his hands regularly with soap. I doubt the monk heard a single word Mark told him.

"Sonam here was one of forty-seven monks taken into the police station," Mark translated. "At first the police used rifle butts and cattle prods to beat all of the monks. Lobsang Gyatso, a twenty-one-year-old monk from Sera Monastery, was beaten on his head with a shovel and fell to the ground inside the police station. Sonam did not see him get up. After the police station began to burn, everyone was taken into the back rooms. The place was getting very hot and Sonam saw a Tibetan policeman let some of the monks escape out a side window. A Chinese policeman saw this and shot the Tibetan policeman in the head with his AK-47. At this time Shue Chuntan, the head police officer, ordered another Chinese policeman to shoot one of the monks in the forehead. His name was Lobsang Deleg, and he was killed instantly. Buchong, a twenty-two-year-old monk from the Jokhang, was also shot. The bullet went in the front and out the back. Both monks were killed with AK-47s. The police told the monks that they had killed a total of eleven people inside and outside the police station. Sonam says the number is really much more, because that doesn't include the Tibetans who will die in prison."

Sonam talked so vehemently that the corners of his mouth were bleeding. This made him look grotesque. He seemed more interested in Heidi's eyes. Heidi realized that the monk had a crush on her and held his hand. Andrew checked to make sure that he had recorded each monk's name, age, and monastery correctly.

"If it weren't for Champa Tenzin," Mark said, referring to the grotesquely burned monk who ran with Sonam inside the burning police station and engaged the police in hand-to-hand combat, "Sonam thinks the police would have killed more people. Sonam and Champa Tenzin created so much commotion that others escaped. The police threatened to shoot anyone who did not exit one of the side windows and run back to the police lines. But after jumping out the window into the side alley, they took a chance and ran toward the Tibetans. He says his face was burned during his escape, and that his burns were minor compared to Champa Tenzin's. This does not bother him compared to a rumor that he has mentioned several times.

"Sonam keeps saying that the police have killed two of the Jokhang monks with lethal injections. The police use two types of injection on the prisoners. One makes the prisoners talk freely. Another makes them crazy, if it does not kill them. He says the injections scare him more than being tortured."

Walking down the main street the next day, I felt as though someone was staring at me and I turned around. People were running to get out of the path of an army convoy of twelve trucks. Each truck had machine guns mounted on its top and cab. At least thirty-five soldiers with fixed bayonets peered menacingly over the side rails of the trucks. Tibetans on the sidewalks made derogatory hand signals and uttered curses under their breath. The caravan of special forces had been sent from Golmud to quell any future uprisings. They had traveled across the Friendship Highway, as we had. With the arrival of reinforcements, snipers appeared on the rooftops around the Jokhang Temple. The soldiers enforced a 10:00 P.M. curfew.

*   *   *

"We were mentioned on the front page of the *New York Times*," John said. "Two days in a row: 'Two Americans arrested in Tibet.'" I had not seen John for two days and thought he was kidding. "I've never been more serious. That piece of paper I sent out with our names and pass-port numbers got on the wire service. Today I talked to correspondents from the *New York Times*, the *Washington Post*, the *Christian Science Monitor*, the *Far Eastern Economic Review*. So many I can't remember. And they all want to speak to the young doctor who is sneaking out to treat the wounded. Andrew is pissed."

John explained that three plane-loads of new arrivals to Lhasa had arrived from Chengdu. The passengers on each plane consisted of mili-tary officers and reporters; both groups were trying to look inconspicu-ous to the other. John said the Chinese were dumb to let the reporters in at all. The reporters didn't sound that smart either—they were all staying at the Lhasa Hotel.

"Can you believe a French magazine is paying an American photographer $600 cash to sneak into Sera Monastery?" John said. "I'd sneak into Sera for free. We should go there tonight. You could treat patients and see a sky burial."

"Do you know what Chinese soldiers did in Sera last night?" I asked.

"No! Do you?"

"They broke in at two in the morning to beat the monks with cattle prods and clubs with nails driven through the ends. The soldiers tried to force the monks to renounce the Dalai Lama and Tibetan independence. After half an hour many of the monks were bleeding profusely. Blood was everywhere. One monk lost his right ear. Several were executed."

"How do you know this?" John asked. "Did the monks tell you? I'd give anything to be able to talk to an eyewitness."

We talked about our respective "tourist" and "medical" undergrounds. John told me about his epic ride back from the Lhasa Hotel at 4:00 A.M., well after curfew, while dogs attacked him.

"I was hoping things would calm down after the riot," John said. "It's just getting worse. All the buses leaving Lhasa this morning were turned back."

Some of the reporters traded bits of information ruthlessly, the way one might trade futures on a commodities exchange. Our story was valuable as an exclusive, if we had not spoken to any other information junkie. If we had, it was worthless. There were also reporters like Ed Gargan of the *New York Times* and Dan Sutherland of the *Washington Post*, who worked hard to get information on the streets instead of at the Lhasa Hotel bar. Tibetans and Westerners working to gather information and help the wounded felt deeply indebted to these and many other reporters whose presence, we felt, protected us.

• • •

A man named Adam who said he was from the State Department arrived in Lhasa with the reporters. Adam was tall, young, and blond, dressed in the khaki pants and upturned collar of an Ivy League preppie.

He bumped into us on the street "accidentally." We talked, and John asked if he could get word to our parents that we were safe. Adam said that he could, if we signed a release of information. I didn't trust Adam. "I advise both of you to leave Lhasa as fast as you can," Adam said. "If something happens, we can't do anything for you. The State Department has no jurisdiction in China."

"We'll be fine," John said. "We've got a week before we have to leave."

"None of my patients are fine," I added, and I told Adam about the twelve confirmed deaths, how wounded Tibetans were afraid to seek medical care at Chinese hospitals, and how monks said that the police were using injections to debilitate recalcitrant prisoners.

"I'll make a note of it in my report," Adam said.

"What is China's official statement about the riot?" John asked.

"The Chinese said that a few splittists staged a small demonstration," Adam said. "They said that Tibetans were angered by what they saw, took guns from the police, and shot the Tibetan demonstrators. The Chinese estimate that one Chinese policeman was killed."

"No police officer was killed," John said. "To the best of my knowledge."

"Leave Tibet now," Adam said. "It's for your own safety."

"What is the State Department's position on the riot?" John challenged.

"China is very sensitive about Tibet," Adam said. "We hope they resolve this incident as soon as possible, but it's not for us to get involved."

• • •

The next afternoon two of our arresting officers, the young Tibetan trying to grow sideburns and the Chinese mute, followed Andrew and me into the market. We were on our way to see a ten-year-old boy who had a fever from an infected gash in his scalp, which he'd gotten when a policeman had struck him with a bayonet during the riot. "I see them," Andrew said after I tipped him off, walking faster. The police were fifty feet behind us. Standing a head taller than the Chinese and Tibetans in the market, we were an easy target for our pursuers. "Follow me,"

Andrew said, zig-zagging between Chinese women selling vegetables. "Shit," Andrew exclaimed, as he splashed through a fetid orange puddle that spanned an alley. We ran down another cobblestone alley where human excrement seeped onto the street from a second-story toilet. A side alley let us sprint around a horse-drawn cart loaded with cabbages. We lost the police and resumed our search for the boy.

Andrew found the boy's house at the back of a construction site, but a stout woman in a purple *chuba* would not let us in. Andrew pleaded with her in Tibetan and Chinese, but she closed the door. I did not blame the woman for not trusting us, but I could not face the boy's dying from infection.

We saw sixteen patients on our second visit to the Jokhang, in a room where beams of light from windows near the high ceiling sliced through the dusty air. The monks were between seventeen and thirty-five years old; all had been beaten severely. After the riot, the police had rounded up twenty Tibetan men, women, and children and took them to an empty schoolhouse. They were beaten for two hours before being released with a warning: "If you demonstrate again, we will kill you."

A pattern to the beatings was obvious: bruises covered each person's head, spine, kidneys, and all the major joints. Nightsticks left long purple bruises on the back and arms. Stones left large, irregular, macerated blotches on the skin. Gun butts left raised triangular patches on the scalp. The external bruises did not bother us as much as the probability of internal bleeding. Even a slow bleed inside the head would increase pressure on the brain until it herniated and the person died. All of the monks complained of headaches, but they were alert, had clear speech, and their pupils responded to light. I knew that several nights later some of them would begin to slur their speech and lapse into coma; I also knew that I was powerless to do anything except document what I had seen.

In exchange for mild pain relievers and reassurance, we were overwhelmed by effusive thanks. Unlike the other monks we had seen inside the Jokhang, no one knew or would tell us the whereabouts of others who had been wounded. As we prepared to leave, I wondered how many more wounded were hiding in Lhasa's homes and monasteries. It was already four days after the riot. People with bullet wounds were dying from infection. Antibiotics were the only lifesaving thing I had to offer.

A nervous young monk came up to Mark and spoke earnestly. Mark translated, "His name is Lobsang. He is concerned about Jokhang monks who were arrested after the riot. He wants us to take their names to the Dalai Lama. Their names are Gyantsen Tharchin Champa Tenzin . . ."

"How many names is that?" Andrew asked.

"One name," Mark said. "You know him. He's the badly burned monk who ran in the police station with Sonam. He was arrested several days after the riot, along with Gampel Sengya, Donyo, and Gamyang Chodon and taken to Sangyip Prison." How could I forget the image of the burned monk, which woke me up in the middle of the night crying?

"Lobsang says that special torture teams from mainland China arrived in Lhasa's prisons after the demonstration. The monks are bound by metal cuffs on the wrist, which get tighter if they move. The cuffs are pounded while the police force the monks to say that Tibet is not free, and find out who organized the demonstrations. Each monk was stripped naked and beaten with clubs with nails driven through the ends, rifle butts, electric cattle prods, and truncheons. Lobsang says the police beat the monks into unconsciousness, then revived them with cold water. No food has been given to them for two days. 'Tibet's freedom will be your food,' one of the policeman yelled at them. Lobsang also says that their testicles were crushed by policemen standing on them."

"How does he know this?" Andrew asked.

"Lobsang tried to visit them in prison. He did not see the monks, but one of the Tibetan guards told him."

"Ask about the special torture teams," Andrew said, taking notes.

Mark translated after he talked with Lobsang for a while: "In addition to their beatings, the prisoners are hung by their thumbs, hung by their ankles upside down with a heater under their head until they pass out, tied to electric beds, and submerged in a tub of ice water. Lobsang says that these tortures were not done before the riot. He also says that he learned that the Austrian secret police helped train the Chinese police."

• • •

"You're under arrest!" a deep voice boomed as the door to my room was kicked open. I sprang into midair with nowhere to run as Julie stepped in. I told her she sounded like she had been taking voice lessons from Tantric chanting monks. Within minutes we were playing hackysack on the Barkhor Square in front of the Jokhang. Hundreds of Tibetans gathered around to witness the spectacle. Julie kicked the hackysack high into the air, to the crowd's astonishment, then let the sack bounce on her raised thigh and down to her feet, where she juggled it with the inside of each foot before passing it to me. The crowd cheered and pushed closer.

A handsome Tibetan Khampa with baggy burlap pants and untied boots stepped into our circle. Julie passed the sack to him and he kicked it hard over her head. The crowd cheered and a flock of children ran screaming after it. The largest boy returned the sack to our circle. He dropped the sack on his foot, juggled it three times expertly, and passed it to Julie. She juggled the sack a few times and passed it to the Khampa. The crowd cheered again as the sack soared over Julie's head.

I realized that we were as much of a spectacle to the Tibetans as the chanting monks were to us. I passed my overturned felt hat. Several Tibetans extricated small, crumpled bank notes worth one cent from folds in their clothes and put them into the hat. One Tibetan woman gave us a two-cent note. A father gave his child a coin to hand to us.

This inspired Julie and me to bring a Tibetan woman into the circle. She juggled the sack several times until the Khampa strode boldly over to her, grabbed the sack, and kicked it back into orbit. The crowd cheered and more crumpled, well-worn notes dropped into the hat. One woman with an infant on her back gave us five cents. The same woman pointed to me and made throwing motions with her arm. Several Tibetans in the crowd mimicked with approval. They must have seen me at the riot. I felt uncomfortable taking any money from a woman with a child on her back, but she wouldn't take it back. It was impossible to get the crowd to step back and give us enough room for more than a minute, impossible for the Khampa not to kick the sack as hard as he could each time he had the chance, impossible not to be awed by Julie's agility. In half an hour we had enough money for a round of beer.

• • •

Mark pulled me off the sidewalk later that afternoon. It was the first time I had ever seen him looking distraught. He said he had just heard my name on Xinhua radio, in Chinese, broadcast from Beijing; it was said that I was a "splittist agent of the Dalai Clique," and that I had urged Tibetans to throw rocks at the police. It was also said that I had been arrested with another foreign instigator and we were being taken to Beijing for further questioning.

"I'm sorry I have to tell you this," Mark said. "I think you should know that Andrew told a reporter and a wire service that you threw rocks at the police during the riot. I couldn't believe he could do such a stupid thing. The damage is done."

I was stunned. I wandered away, and I'm not sure if I even said good-bye to Mark. Telling reporters that I had thrown rocks at the police jeopardized my being able to sneak out for medical rounds. Andrew had no reason to give anyone my name, unless he wanted to hurt me. I could feel myself exploding as my hotel loomed larger in front of my eyes. I found Andrew on the third-floor balcony, talking with John and a core group of travelers I recognized from the first meeting after the riot. Andrew didn't wait for me to reach him before leaving the meeting. "Let's talk in your room, shall we?" he said.

"Did you tell the reporters I threw rocks?" I exploded as soon as we were in my room.

"No," Andrew said, sitting down calmly on the bed.

"Don't lie to me," I shouted. "Did you tell reporters I threw rocks at the police?"

"Who told you this?" Andrew said, as though talking to a child. I yelled at him and he moved farther back on the bed.

John came in then and told Andrew, "Blake is easily excited. You should have seen how hyper he got when we were arrested." He asked in a nonjudgmental tone if Andrew had told a reporter that I had thrown rocks. Andrew squirmed.

"Did you?" I yelled before John could intervene.

"Well . . ." Andrew stammered, ". . . yes, I did."

"*Why?*"

"Because you *did* throw rocks."

"Don't you see how that jeopardizes Blake's staying in Lhasa?" John interjected.

It became clear why Andrew wanted me out of the picture. The reporters had been more interested in talking to us than to Andrew, the self-proclaimed leader of the "tourist underground." He was jealous. This was a brilliant way to get rid of me. My right fist tightened into a knot. I thought how good it would feel to punch Andrew, especially with his glasses on. "I'd like to punch you in the mouth," I told him.

"Are you threatening me?" Andrew asked.

"No—yes, goddamnit! I could be arrested again."

"Well, calm down," Andrew said. "We have to work together. We have to get medicine to Champa Tenzin."

CHAPTER NINE

SKY BURIAL

TERRY'S PARTIES WERE well known to Lhasa's overland travelers. An alcoholic and polysubstance abuser who
smoked opium to wean himself from intravenous heroin, Terry
cultivated the appearance of a suicidal clown: black eye-liner running
into hastily applied rouge, electric lavender and orange pajamas, and a
shawl draped protectively around his shoulders. He was fastidious about
ensuring that he acquired all of the essential ingredients for a successful
bash. Tonight he was proud to be offering forty liters of Tibetan *chang.*

Because of the 10:00 P.M. curfew, people began arriving before dark
and filled the hall at the Banak Shol's rear perimeter. German punk,
Japanese new wave, and English rock and roll blasted out over the
Tibetan homes in the Barkhor. From a balcony I surveyed the moonlit
clotheslines of socks and underwear in the courtyard and the hallway
that led to our rooms. I was convinced that the police would come to
arrest us, and that I would have to climb over the hotel's rear wall. John
said I was being histrionic. I no longer found any glamour in the idea of
an overland escape.

"Come in before you freeze to death," John said from inside the hall.
I didn't answer. He and Otto climbed out the window to join me on the
balcony, and I listened to them discuss a demonstration John had seen
today at the post office. Eighty monks from Drepung Monastery
dressed in civilian clothes marched all the way into town before being
discovered. Four trucks of soldiers drove past them on the way to the
monastery. When the soldiers arrived at Drepung and realized their
mistake, they raced back into town. According to Otto, the soldiers

found the monks in front of the post office, beat them with cattle prods and rifle butts, and carted the limp bodies away in the trucks. John said that he hadn't seen anyone unconscious.

"I was afraid to take pictures," John said. "A woman next to me got her film taken."

John's description of the demonstration prompted toasts to the Tibetan freedom fighters. "We will have a travelers' demonstration," Otto said.

"No more politics tonight," Terry said from inside the hall. "We have forty liters of *chang* to drink."

John's story of the beaten monks blended with the details of my day: another boy dying of sepsis whose parents were afraid to let us into their home; a forty-seven-year-old woman shot in the breast; and a sixty-eight-year-old man who had been shot from a rooftop. We also learned of an imprisoned monk who had suffered a compound fracture of his right arm during a torture session.

"The Chinese are even crueler than the Americans," Otto said. "I would like to shoot the police. Maybe I steal an AK-47."

I heard the sound of glass shattering as a rock crashed through a window above the tape player. This didn't stop the blaring music. Like Otto, I had thought of killing. During the riot I had imagined getting a gun. When I was charging at the police, I don't know what I would have done with a gun if I had gotten one, but I knew that I had wanted to kill. This realization frightened me more than the idea of being shot. My life and training as a physician had taught me to respect all life. Now I feared I was becoming obsessed with the thought of taking life.

"A toast to Otto," John said. "We won't see him again if he's shot by the Chinese police."

More toasts, and curses at the rock thrower, accompanied the music that continued to bombard the Barkhor. It occurred to me that the stone thrower may have been hiding someone wounded during the riot; perhaps they just wanted to sleep. I wanted to enjoy myself at the party and felt jealous that I could not relax. I also felt repulsed by Westerners enjoying themselves while Tibetans were dying.

From the balcony we watched as, across the courtyard, four of the five policeman who had arrested John and me—the mute, two deputies, and the young Tibetan trying to grow sideburns—walked down a hall and knocked at our door, which John had padlocked. "Now do you believe it?" I challenged John.

We saw a young Tibetan man sprint conspicuously along a third-floor balcony above the police, slide down a corrugated metal roof, and lower himself into the courtyard. The brilliant moon illuminated his frenetic dash through the clotheslines and his ascent up a ladder to our balcony. He moved with the awkward intensity of an animal that was about to be slaughtered. Breathless, he told us his name was Namgyal. I wondered if he was working with the Tibetan underground.

"Very bad men," Namgyal said, flipping his pinky up. *Chang* perfumed his breath and slurred his speech.

"Why are the police here?" John asked.

"All foreigners must leave Lhasa. The police have developed their film of the riot. They will arrest everyone involved. Everyone." Namgyal left as frantically as he had come, reversing his route down the ladder into the courtyard. The police were sure to see him.

"Let's leave," I implored John.

"You can leave if you want to," John said. "We're getting more *chang*." Otto and John climbed back inside, leaving me alone to brood out in the cold.

"You're under arrest!" a deep voice boomed. I jumped and looked around frantically—there was nowhere to run on the balcony. Then Julie appeared, smiling, climbing out the window. "Nice trick," I said, shivering. She covered me with a blanket and we hid in the shadows. The four police officers came four different times to our room, and four times an acid knife gouged at my stomach as they pounded and yelled at the door. But for some reason they never tried to break in, nor did they come to look for us at the party. "They're afraid of us," John boasted later, but I wasn't inclined to take unnecessary chances. I cursed him for staying here tonight, and for making me realize that I could not leave, either. When the police finally left the hotel at four, Julie and I went into our room, made love, and fell asleep, while John and the others partied through the night.

• • •

"The police came to our hotel last night. They were checking visas," Mark said at the next morning's medical meeting. He sat next to Heidi, their arms and legs touching. "I didn't care that my visa had expired," Mark said, "but all of our extra medicines were under the bed. I stayed under the covers and pretended to be sick. I said I had been vomiting and had violent diarrhea. They ordered me to leave as soon as I could travel. I'm going to sleep at a safe house tonight. You are all welcome to stay there if you want."

Mark described the house of a Tibetan friend of his. It reminded me of the home of Carolyn's Tibetan family, but nothing about it sounded safe—especially when Andrew said that he would stay there. That night Julie and I snuck into a different hotel's dormitory for a catnap and left before the hotel employees woke up. If we were caught, I reasoned, it would be better for the hotel if we had not registered.

Mark and Heidi met a man named Tenzin in the Barkhor, who led me to Lodi, another gunshot victim from the riot. Tenzin was so nervous that he made me nervous. His pinstriped suit seemed an anachronism in the Barkhor. When we got to Lodi's house, Tenzin said that after Lodi was shot in the calf, the police had taken him to the People's Hospital, where a Chinese surgeon removed the bullet. I told him that I had not heard of any wounded Tibetans receiving medical care at the People's Hospital.

"After the surgeon finished sewing the wound," Tenzin replied, "Lodi ran away. Otherwise the police would have taken him to prison."

Lodi sat in a chair with both legs on a stool. I later learned he was twenty-six years old, but a fever and taut facial muscles made him look much older. Lodi looked so ill that I barely noticed a petite Tibetan woman with us, who I assumed was his daughter. Lodi's wound was badly infected. The sutures had to be cut and the abscess drained or he would die from sepsis.

Lodi laughed and I asked what was so funny. "Lodi says he must have very bad luck," Tenzin said. "He sprained his good ankle when he was running away from the police."

"Lodi has good luck not to be in prison," I said.

Lodi repeated three times that he would have done anything to avoid going to prison. He had heard about the special torture teams that had come from Chengdu to Lhasa's Gutsa Prison, which used new electrical devices on Tibetan prisoners. He asked why I washed my hands, and I gave him a graphic description of great "Kali germs" that destroy all neighboring flesh unless you take "special pills" that His Holiness also takes when he gets sick.

"*Dalai Lama yakbudoo*," Lodi said as I cut his sutures, to a rush of foul-smelling pus.

"*Dalai Lama yakbudoo*," I said. Lodi winced as I irrigated the pus from the wound. I explained how the "special pills" circulated in the blood, and why his daughter had to wash her hands before she changed his bandage.

Tenzin said that the nineteen-year-old "daughter" was Lodi's wife, Kunyang. She had a terrible skin infection that had not gone away for over one year. The Tibetan doctors at the *Mendzekhang* had tried many different medicines. None had any effect, until they tried penicillin. Now the infection was improving. I asked Kunyang how many children she had and she looked down in shame. I looked to Tenzin to see what I had said wrong. He looked away.

With tears in her eyes, Kunyang talked softly in Tibetan. Tenzin translated: "Last year, Kunyang was six months' pregnant. The work unit leader saw that she was showing and ordered her to go to the People's Hospital for a checkup. Inside the hospital, the Chinese doctor said that she needed an operation to save her life. Kunyang insisted that she was healthy. She argued with the doctors but it was no use. The nurse injected her belly with something that made the baby come out. She heard the baby cry. Then the nurse gave an injection into the soft spot on the baby's forehead. The next day Kunyang was forced to have an operation. She says she cannot have any more children."

* * *

"Give me your medical bag," Andrew demanded the next afternoon. He looked delighted. "It's not fair to your patients. You're too high-profile. The police have come to your room two days in a row. The streets are teeming with army and undercover police."

I gave Andrew my shoulder bag. Instead of yelling at him I wanted to cry. The truth was that it would be a relief not to sneak out to see patients. Like the wounded Tibetans I had snuck out to treat, I had also become a fugitive. I was afraid to stay in Lhasa and afraid to go back to my hotel in case the police were there. I was afraid of my patients dying from infection and afraid to go to their homes in case we were seen. Stripped of my medicine bag, I could no longer hide behind the brave image of a physician helping the wounded.

More than explicit violence, I was afraid of the implicit violence in Tibet's military occupation: the wounded being sent to prison; the routine torture of prisoners; women entering Chinese hospitals for checkups and being forced to have abortions and be sterilized. I was also afraid for those Tibetans who remembered their country before the Chinese invaded, and for the two generations of children who had grown up in fear.

* * *

On what I thought might be our last night together, Julie and I went to an after-hours bar packed with other Westerners who had decided to stay in Lhasa as long as they could. We held hands under the table. Heidi had her arm around Mark. John cuddled a puppy in his lap. "Her name is Rangzen," John said. "I found her on the street. Rangzen means freedom in Tibetan."

"Him," I corrected, inspecting the dog's genitals.

John stroked the puppy affectionately. "I wonder where Rangzen and I will sleep tonight."

"I saw a man get dragged out of his house this afternoon," Julie said. "On the main street. Six policemen beat him unconscious with their rifles. I heard his head crack."

"This afternoon I saw a Tibetan man swerve his bicycle in front of a police jeep," Mark said. "The driver had to swerve and slammed on the brakes. He jumped out and beat the man to the ground with a truncheon. Then a fat man got out of the jeep with his pistol drawn. He stepped on the Tibetan's neck and put the pistol to his head, the whole time yelling in Chinese. 'Shoot me,' I yelled, 'Shoot me, you bastard,' until the police got back in their jeep and drove off."

"We have to get out of here," John said.

"You've got to get your film out," Julie said.

"The first scheduled commercial flight to Kathmandu is leaving in

two days," John said. "A bus leaves from the Lhasa Hotel to the airport
at four in the morning. We could dress in clean clothes. The police
won't expect us to be mixed in with the Holiday Inn tourists, and that
crowd doesn't get searched."

An Australian man at an adjacent table pulled a lubricated condom
over his head, which squashed his eyes shut and flattened his nose. He
gulped air through his mouth and exhaled through his nose to inflate
the condom like a balloon. His table of fellow Australians stamped their
feet and banged their fists and their countryman's neck and cheeks
turned scarlet, as the tip of the condom swelled to basketball size and
exploded.

Out on the empty street, John ripped the latest in a series of official
announcements off a wall:

*The No. 3 Announcement by the People's
Government of the City of Lhasa*

In order to ensure the smooth implementation of the opening
police, to promote the development of tourism industry in our
region, to increase our economic and technical exchange and co-
operation with different countries in the World, to avoid appearance of displeasure in foreign affairs's work, the city announces as
follows:

1.   We extend welcome to friends from the different countries in
     the World who come to our region for sightseeing, tour, visit,
     work, trade discussion and economic cooperation.
2.   Who ever comes to our region must *respects* our State sover-
     eignty, abide by the *lows* of our country. They are not allowed
     to interfere in internal affairs of our country and engage in
     activities that are incompatible with their status.
3.   Foreigners are not allowed to crowd around watching and
     photographing the disturbances manipulated by a few split-
     tists, and they should not do any distorted propaganda con-
     cerning disturbances, which is not in agreement with the
     facts.
4.   In accordance with our *lows*, we shall mete out punishment

to the trouble-makers who stir up, support and participate in the disturbance manipulated by a few splittists.

Mark, Heidi, Julie, Otto, John, Rangzen, two fellow inebriated travelers, and I all proceeded to rip down every Chinese poster in the Barkhor, in defiance of the local *lows*. We stopped outside the Kiri Hotel's two-story metal gate, which had been locked for the night. Climbing the gate would have been a formidable task when sober. Instead we played hackysack under the streetlight.

A rock skidded through our group. We could barely make out three silhouettes fifty yards away next to a vehicle. I stopped the next rock with my foot. They couldn't throw far enough to hit us directly. John picked up a rock. So did Otto, Julie, and the two travelers. "One, two, three," I whispered, and we launched a collective volley with no thought of the consequences. Our rocks, too, fell far short of our target. The silhouettes jumped into the vehicle, which backlit their dome-shaped helmets. We froze in the approaching headlights.

The two travelers ran down a side alley. Julie and I scrambled over the gate and sprinted across the courtyard. Mark, John, Heidi, and Otto followed. The vehicle stopped outside the gate. The police got out and yelled for the gatekeeper as a flashlight beam probed the dark recesses of the courtyard. Julie and I hid in the toilets. The gatekeeper would have to let the police in. They would wake up every traveler and tear the hotel apart. How could we have been so stupid? I held my breath and stared between the horribly stained porcelain foot pads. I never thought I could have hidden in a Tibetan toilet, even if it meant avoiding prison. I was naive. Julie and I huddled there for hours, unsure if the police had left. We did not see the others again until morning.

* * *

I felt no animosity toward Andrew when we met for the last time to talk about our patients, only sadness for how little I had been able to do for the wounded. As a direct result of gunshot wounds and beatings during the October 1 riot, we had confirmed twelve deaths. We also had documented fourteen Tibetans with bullet wounds, two monks with burns, and fifty Tibetans with multiple contusions from severe beatings.

Andrew fastidiously recorded the name, sex, and age of each patient, the location of entrance and exit wounds, course of treatment, and prognosis. He also recorded details about four monks who were still missing from the Jokhang, two monks believed to have been killed by lethal injection, and the eighty monks from Drepung Monastery who were clubbed with cattle prods and AK-47s before being taken to prison.

Andrew thanked me for what I had done and said that he would stay as long as he could to collect the names of Tibetan prisoners. At that moment, standing in the street and wishing Andrew luck, I realized the importance of his forty-five-page handwritten document for the press. I admired his tenacity and his obsessive attention to detail. Andrew smiled and excused himself abruptly.

"There's a monk dying in the Jokhang," Julie said the next afternoon. "A monk approached me in the market. He said the police hit his friend many times on the head during the riot. Two days ago he started losing coordination. The monks didn't think anything of it. Then his speech became slurred. Now he's unconscious."

What Julie described was called a subdural hematoma. The police had hit the monk's head hard enough to break a blood vessel in his brain, which continued to bleed. The monk needed a hole bored in his skull to relieve the pressure. The thought of the monk's brain being squeezed against the inside of his skull made me shudder. So did the thought of trying to perform a trephination with a Swiss Army knife. "There's nothing I can do," I said. "Even if—"

Julie pulled a Dalai Lama postcard from the back pocket of her jeans. "If he can still see, we can hold a picture of His Holiness as an offering," she said. Julie was right. I felt embarrassed for hesitating. I was so tired that the thought of getting arrested seemed appealing; at least then I could relax.

We walked arm in arm through the Barkhor Square, where snipers with binoculars and telephoto lenses occupied the rooftops. Before completing a circuit around the Jokhang, we slipped into a close-by construction site. Chinese workers stopped laying bricks to giggle at the two lovers stealing up a bamboo ladder into the depths of an unfinished building. We continued to a back window that let us onto one of the Jokhang's rooftops. After crossing several terraces, we dropped onto Lobsang's balcony.

Lobsang jumped when we stepped into his room. It was reassuring to see his face. Shadows from seven butter lamps leapt across the walls as I used my rudimentary Tibetan and sign language to describe Julie's unconscious monk. Lobsang did not understand and left us alone in his quarters. Sitting quietly on the hard bench, I realized that I was bored. So much had already happened to us in Lhasa that I now needed the adrenaline rush I had become used to getting on a regular basis.

Lobsang returned with Tashi, a monk from Amdo who spoke English. "No one has heard of an unconscious monk," Tashi translated. "The police are preparing to storm the Jokhang. They have done this many times, sometimes killing monks. It is dangerous for you here. You have to leave. Lobsang wants you to take a message to His Holiness."

Lobsang looked at me quizzically and laughed. I asked why and Tashi said, "He's waiting for you to take notes." I pulled a four-by-four-inch bandage wrapper from my pocket and tried to write fast enough to keep up with Tashi's translating. "Puchong was shot through the left chest inside the police station on October 1," Tashi said. "Lobsang went to get the body with some of the other monks two days ago. When he asked for the body, the police demanded 650 yuan. Lobsang said monks did not have that kind of money. The police wrote their names down in a book and said if they didn't bring the money the next day they would all go to prison.

"Lobsang came back with the money," Tashi continued. "Puchong's hands were still tied behind his back. One bullet went through his chest. Another went through the stomach. The back of his head was crushed. Large bruises covered his kidneys. There were many bruises and cuts on all limbs. Puchong's body went to Sera for sky burial. Do you have all this down?"

Writing down what Tashi translated wasn't the problem. Reading it would be. Lobsang stopped talking and Julie asked if he had heard of any women in prison. Lobsang started talking again at high speed.

"For participating in the October 1 demonstration, Namla was taken to Gutsa Prison on the same day. She is only twenty-three years old, from Garu nunnery. The police stripped her and beat her with sticks with nails in the ends, rifle butts, and electric sticks. They also beat her while she was hanging from her ankles with a heater placed under her head, for hours. The police tied her to an electric bed, and tied an electric belt around her breasts." Tashi stopped translating and giggled with embarrassed discomfort. I asked what was funny and he said, "The police jabbed the electric stick into Namla's vagina."

I asked Tashi how Lobsang had come to know all of this. He said that Lobsang knew the woman's sister well. I looked for another scrap of paper to write on and Lobsang unfurled two white silk *khatas* and put them over our necks.

"Lobsang thanks both of you for what you have done for the Tibetan people," Tashi said. "He says that he will never forget you. He asks you to please tell the Dalai Lama what is happening to his country."

• • •

Like many Westerners who had seen the riot, Julie had decided not to leave, but to stay as long as she could to gather more information. The mobile loudspeakers broadcast in the streets that the authorities would be "lenient" with Tibetans who participated in the demonstration. Criminals who didn't give themselves up would be "punished." Julie and I planned to meet again somewhere, in Nepal, India, or back in the States. We told each other how much we wished we had more time together. We exchanged addresses and phone numbers and wept on each other's shoulders as we hugged.

John and I took showers, shaved, and washed our clothes, the better to blend in with the tourists at the airport. Before walking to the bus, which left at 2:00 A.M., John hid rolls of film in his dirty socks and underwear and scattered condoms throughout his pack, in an attempt to distract soldiers at the airport customs. We fought continuously during the hour-long walk to the Lhasa Hotel, but we agreed to pretend that we did not know each other at the airport; if the police held one of us back, the other would try to keep going. Four soldiers got on the bus with us.

At 6:00 A.M. the bus droned steadily up the Lhasa valley. The Tibetan homes and fields of barley in the valley seemed impossibly far away from the tumult of the demonstrations. A donkey stood unattended in a stream. Smoke curled out of an adobe house. A British couple complained that the bus was taking too long, and then we had to wait in line while soldiers checked each passport individually. I went before

John. Two male soldiers perused my passport and handed it to a woman, who noticed the canceled visa. She yelled at the men for what they had missed.

"Why canceled?" she demanded angrily.

"I made cheese out of yogurt to sell to tourists," I said. "I had to pay a fine."

"How much fine?"

"Fifty FEC."

The woman's professionally angry demeanor cracked. She smiled as though this had been an appropriate punishment and said, "I hope you learn from this lesson." She waved me on. "Stop," a soldier yelled. I spun around and the woman pointed to the airport tax counter. I was so happy to pay the airport tax that I didn't even mind waiting for John to get through customs.

John looked nervous when he handed his passport to the male soldiers. Once again, they both missed the canceled visa and the woman yelled at them. I imagined John being led away. He said something I couldn't hear and they waved him through. "They didn't even search me," John said after he paid the airport tax. "She asked me why my visa was canceled. Naturally, I told her the truth, that you had thrown rocks at the police—"

"John!" I exclaimed loud enough to startle a couple next to us.

"You would make a terrible secret agent," John said. "I told her I had changed 100 FEC for yuan on the black market. She wanted to know how much I was fined. I said thirty FEC and she said that wasn't bad. Someone else was fined fifty FEC for selling homemade cheese to tourists."

We waited another hour for the rest of the passengers to be processed through customs, another hour for a bus that took us to the plane, and thirty minutes standing on the tarmac while soldiers walked up and down the line, intimidating each passenger. Amid this final display of force, I noticed three sleek black helicopters with exaggerated blades stationed farther down the runway.

Instead of being ecstatic when the plane took off, John and I sat on separate sides of the cabin. As the snowcapped Himalayas passed beneath us, I wondered how many Tibetans were trying to escape across the mountains at that moment. What would happen to the burned monk? How many wounded Tibetans would die in their homes? How many people were being tortured in prisons? I felt defeated thinking of the ten-year-old boy who would die soon from infection. Up to now in my life I had always thought that living would be better than dying, no matter what. I had never seen children slaughtered in the street. I had never met monks tortured in prison and women sterilized against their will. In a moment of despair, I wondered if the Tibetan boy would be better off dying than living under Chinese military occupation.

I looked back at John and saw him staring out the window. I cried in fitful, uncontrollable sobs, and envisioned the body of a dead monk lying on a boulder. It was Puchong, Lobsang's friend. Large, ugly bruises covered the corpse, which had been shot once in the chest and once in the abdomen. The wrists were still tied behind the back.

When the sun hit the rock, the body breakers stopped drinking *chang* and began to hack flesh from the corpse. They chopped the body into small pieces and crushed the bones. Vultures waited patiently at the crest of the hill. Clotted blood spilled onto the rock and over the hands of the body breakers, who worked quickly, without pause, to prepare their celestial offering. In Tibet's high-altitude desert, with little wood for cremation and burial reserved for criminals whose souls should not be reborn, sky burial was a practical solution to the problem of death's decay. Once the flesh and bones were mixed with barley flour, the sky became dark with enormous black wings as the vultures descended upon their corporeal feast.

CHAPTER TEN

WHAT DO WE TELL THE CHILDREN?

KATHMANDU WELCOMED US with an extravagance of foliage, colors, and smells that was a stark contrast to desert-like Tibet. The taxi's two-tone horn parted the sea of pedestrians as we sped past glass shelves heaped with pies, chocolate cakes, cookies, and slabs of dark chocolate. Indian, French, Mexican, Italian, Greek, Vietnamese, and Tibetan restaurants beckoned. Rock-and-roll bars provided a backdrop for street urchins, skeleton-like cows, and a legless man pushing himself on a skateboard.

The desk manager of the Tibetan Hotel gave us a room for half price when he learned we were the "American doctor and lawyer arrested in Tibet." He also said we could make overseas calls at the hotel's rate. Before our calls to our families went through, though, we had a visitor.

"Dr. Kerr and Mr. Ackerly?" said a large, distinguished-looking man wearing a white linen suit. "Please allow me to introduce myself. My name is Kedar Man Singh. I am Kathmandu's official Associated Press representative. I am also the Association Francaise Presse correspondent."

Singh shook his head from side to side as he talked. "You are famous, really. The whole world is waiting for your story. I would like to take your picture and send your story on the AP wire as soon as possible."

Neither John nor I knew what to say. Singh kept talking. "There is much for you to do in Kathmandu. I am personally knowing the BBC man here. He is a very good fellow who also wants to take your photo and interview you. Tibet is a big issue in your country right now. You were in all the papers and magazines."

"We're in more trouble than I thought," I whispered to John, mimicking Singh's accent and shaking my head from side to side. "I have 108 hours of sleep to catch up on."

Singh wanted us to wear our packs for the picture. I also wanted to wear my wide-brimmed felt hat that smelled of yak butter and carried the many hues of the Tibetan landscape. We compromised and took two pictures, one with packs and hat and one without.

"What is happening in Tibet now you will not see mentioned favorably in our press," Singh said. "The Nepalese are afraid of China. We have had border disputes with China since 1962. It is an explosive issue. And why is Nepal so afraid to say the least little bit of criticism about China? Nepal has very big mountains, but it is a very small country. And China's army is so big!"

* * *

"I'm so happy you're alive," my mother said, crying through the long-distance crackle on the other end of the phone. I said that we were safe in Kathmandu, and that I would be home once I gained thirty pounds. "We heard you were arrested. Then the police station burned down. I thought you were killed." Her voice faded into sobs.

"It was a different police station," I said, trying to sound reassuring.

"I'm so glad you're safe. I'll call the Ackerlys right away." My mother explained that Michael Van Walt, the Dalai Lama's lawyer, wanted us to testify at a congressional hearing on human rights violations in Tibet. We had to fly to Washington, D.C., as soon as possible. John's parents and my mother would meet our flight. "I don't suppose you brought a suit, so we'll bring them. You and John are heroes to the Tibetan people. That's what Rinchen Darlo, the U.S. representative for the Dalai Lama, said." I didn't feel like a hero, or able to cope with any new impositions on my life.

Then she added, "The Dalai Lama wants to see you. Do you have a pen? I'll give you the numbers of the Kathmandu and Delhi offices of Tibet. They are hoping to hear from you as soon as possible."

"John!" I yelled. "The Dalai Lama wants to see us!"

* * *

Paljor Tsering, the Tibetan government-in-exile's representative in Nepal, sent a car to bring us to the Tibetan Consulate. Hidden from the street behind a high brick wall, a grapefruit tree on the spacious lawn had so much ripe yellow fruit that each branch bowed to the ground.

"I would like to get your impressions of what you have seen in Tibet on video while they are still fresh," Paljor said. He offered us tea. "Perhaps tomorrow. His Holiness will see the video before you meet him. I have already telexed Delhi. They are preparing for your arrival. His Holiness is very interested in what happened in the riots and the demonstrations. He wants to thank you personally for all you have done to help the Tibetan people."

"How was the riot portrayed in the Nepalese press?" John asked.

"I saved all the articles," Paljor said. "Many mention you. The Chinese government says that you are splittist agents of the Dalai clique. They said you threw rocks at the police and urged the Tibetans to attack the police station."

"What about the police shooting unarmed people?" I asked.

"The articles didn't mention that."

"That's ridiculous," John said.

"Of course it is. The Nepalese press says whatever China tells it to say. This is a difficult time for Tibetans. You have seen for yourselves what happens to Tibetans in Tibet who demonstrate for independence. Until the riots China was very successful at preventing any information from getting out of Tibet. Tibetans in exile wait for tidbits of news.

"Even in Kathmandu," Paljor continued, "I am not free to say what is really happening in Tibet. The Nepalese government is angered by what has come out in the press. Two days ago an article accused a Tibetan youth organization of threatening to bomb the Nepalese Embassy. This is of course not true. I am in a difficult situation. That is why we are so happy to see the two of you. You are free to say what is really happening in Tibet. But even you have to be careful. The Nepalese may kick you out of the country if you make political statements."

* * *

The next three days were packed with lengthy video interviews with Paljor Tsering and French and Dutch television, talking long-distance to CBS News, and sending a detailed, fifty-minute telex concerning the riot and the individuals killed and wounded to the Senate Foreign Relations Committee. Nightmares and being woken up by an otherwise pleasant woman from National Public Radio at 2:00 A.M.—twice—precluded my getting more than two hours of consecutive sleep. We were so busy we forgot to get our Indian visas until the day before our press conference in Delhi.

When we got to the Indian Embassy, thirty Westerners were waiting impatiently at the visa window. When John asked for visa applications, the guard said, "Come back tomorrow." John persisted and got two applications, which we filled out and handed back. "You see these people?" the guard said. "You have to bring your application back tomorrow, like these people have done. The day after that you will get your visas. Not before."

"We have to be in Delhi tomorrow," John pleaded.

"Show me your tickets."

"We don't have them yet," John said. "We were going to get them after we got our visas."

"There is nothing I can do."

"What if we get our plane tickets and come back?" John asked.

"It is no use. Come back tomorrow."

"We have a press conference in New Delhi tomorrow," John said.

"You are not looking like a press conference. This is a civilized country we are living in. I am telling you, tomorrow is tomorrow."

"Why can't you take our applications today?" John demanded.

"It is no use arguing. Nothing can be done. I assure you."

Two prior trips to India had taught me the futility of getting mad at government officials. The country's institutionalized inefficiency made Westerners like John and me go berserk. The trick was to discover something that the official wanted; money usually sufficed as a last resort. I approached the man calmly and whispered, "We are coming from Tibet."

"Why didn't you say you were coming from Tibet?" The guard walked down a freshly raked gravel path through a garden to a building surrounded by Gurkha soldiers and manicured lawn. He returned promptly. "My superior officer will see you now."

"I will be honest with you if you will be honest with me," a large army officer said, stretching his pudgy hands to the edge of the desk. He wore a green khaki uniform with the collar unbuttoned. "As you men know, the Nepalese are interested in China's military presence in Tibet. Naturally, with you just coming from Lhasa, you have seen things that would be useful to us. I will get right to the point. If you write down everything you saw about China's army and air force at Gonggar Airport, I will arrange to have your visas ready by five o'clock."

The officer leaned forward to inspect my crude drawing of a sleek helicopter with exaggerated propellers. "Sikorsky helicopters from America!" the officer exclaimed. "Write it all down. Come back at five."

"I don't trust him," John said outside the consulate. "He told us to come back an hour after they close.

"Relax," I said, mimicking John. "A few drawings and troop estimates and we meet the Dalai Lama. Jesus—what are we going to call him?"

• • •

"Who started the riot?"

"Why did you throw rocks?"

"Are you working for the CIA?"

These were three simultaneous questions from reporters at the New Delhi press conference. We were trapped at the back of a room where eighty reporters were clamoring to ask us questions. The air conditioning didn't work. The room was so humid that beads of water trickled down the wallpaper. Forgetting that we were in a hotel in Delhi, where even the air could give me dysentery, I guzzled ice water.

"Are you a military expert?" shouted one reporter, whom we later learned represented the city's communist paper.

"Were you ever in the military?"

"Did the Tibetans have guns?"

"Why did you even talk to Tibetans?"

I was so nervous I spilled my glass of water into a nest of wires, microphones, and tape recorders on the white tablecloth. Two waiters in white coats brought fresh glasses of water and towels to mop up the spill. No one was electrocuted. John and I forsook our prepared statements and tried our best to answer the aggressive barrage:

"How many people were killed?"

"How many were wounded?"

"Why did the Tibetans kill a Chinese policeman if they're pacifists?"

"What about the public execution? First the Chinese said three were executed, then two."

"How many foreigners were in Lhasa at the time?"

"How many saw the riot?"

"There were hundreds of Westerners in Lhasa," John said, trying to keep up. "Dozens of foreigners must have witnessed the riot. It was widely felt that there would have been a massacre if the foreigners had not been present in such great numbers in the crowd."

"Why did you throw rocks at the police?"

"I did not throw rocks at the police," John said. "I took photographs."

"What is China's military presence at the border?"

"We flew over the border," I said.

"What is the condition of the Tibetans versus the Chinese?"

"The Tibetans live under military occupation," I said. "Chinese is the official language of government and industry. Monks do not have religious freedom. Children don't learn Tibetan in schools. Protesters are tortured."

"Mr. Ackerly, what is your view of the whole thing?"

"What the Chinese are doing in Tibet has already happened in Inner Mongolia and Xinjian, the old East Turkestan," John said. "It's a racial situation. No matter how you feel about Tibet's autonomy, the Tibetan language and culture have always been separate from China's. Some of the policies of the Cultural Revolution are still going on, and Chinese colonization in Tibet is a serious threat to their culture."

"What will happen to Tibet?"

"As long as the Tibetans are treated as second-class citizens in their own land, there will be revolts."

One hour of questions whizzed by and we found ourselves being served a sumptuous feast of chicken and lamb curries, dal bat, yogurt, and salad. Everyone shook our hands and assured us that we had done a good job.

•   •   •

We played rummy on the floor of the Old Delhi train station while waiting for the 5:00 A.M. train to Dharamsala, home of the Dalai Lama and the Tibetan government-in-exile. Hundreds of skeletal Indians slept on the platform surrounding us, their gaunt cheeks and hollow eyes at peace for a few hours. The fortunate had a blanket or piece of cloth to lie on. A deformed boy held my hand as we played. My arms were bigger than his legs. Two of my fingers were wider than his arm. He had no neck and his jaw rested on top of his chest, which was pinched forward into a grotesque prow. We let him shuffle the cards and deal.

We glimpsed the Indian countryside on the train from New Delhi to Petan Court. As the sun burned through the layers of mist that blanketed the fields, we saw Indians squatting on cracked, parched earth. Children splashed in a muddy trickle of water that meandered through a desiccated river bed. Deprived of this year's monsoon, India was left hot but not humid; the rains had gone north of the Himalayas to Tibet. The papers also reported a 99.9 percent crop failure in India's southern provinces. The bleak forecast of famine in a country where 15 million children starve to death every year had a sobering effect on our journey.

* * *

A young Tibetan had been sent from Dharamsala to pick us up at Petan Court train station. We left the arid plains and started winding toward the snowcapped foothills of the Himalayas. I had wanted to meet the Dalai Lama for fifteen years, but never thought it would be possible. I am neither an avowed Buddhist nor a statesman. My lifestyle is far from holy. The prospect of meeting the Dalai Lama made me so nervous I decided to write down questions to ask him. I got stuck on the first one: What do you think about foreigners in Tibet throwing rocks at the police?

"Are you sure you want to tell the Dalai Lama about throwing rocks?" John said, ever the lawyerly strategist.

"With all the media attention we're getting, he has to know who he's dealing with."

"Just because you have a guilty conscience doesn't mean you have to tell him everything. This won't be a confession."

"If I don't tell him I'll regret it later."

Dharamsala had changed since I had visited the old British Hill station seven years earlier during a trip to India. The mountains still leapt off the subcontinent, but more houses covered the hillside. Deep cuts from erosion scarred the mature pine forest on the hillside.

We stopped for a troop of monkeys sitting on the road, their red rumps high in the air as they sauntered across the strip of asphalt intruding on their forest. Young monkeys clung upside down to their mothers' fur as tenaciously as the trees clung to the steep scree slope. The largest male berated our jeep with a bone-chilling cry, stared it down to a standstill, then dragged his pendulous red testicles into the trees.

• • •

Thubten Samphel greeted us at the Information Office with cups of sweet tea and effusive thanks. "We do not wish to impose on your time," Thubten said, "but many of the younger Tibetans at the children's village have never seen Tibet. You have seen more of their country than they have, and they are Tibetan. We have 800 children eight to seventeen years old. We didn't used to have so many. Ten years ago many of our children were orphans. Their parents were killed by the Chinese army in Tibet, or else while trying to escape. Sometimes women come out of Tibet to have their baby here, then return; if they do not, their families will be suspect.

"We try to give the children Tibetan and Western educations," Thubten continued. "They study Tibetan, English, religious texts, science, and mathematics. Soon we will be getting a computer. If you would share your impressions of Tibet with some of the organizations in Dharamsala, it would mean so much to them. Many of the older Tibetans are anxious for any news of their homeland. We will provide you with a jeep and driver."

John and I both smiled at the thought of a jeep to drive us around. "It would be our privilege," John said.

Thubten beamed. "Then tomorrow you will give a talk at the Tibetan Children's Village at ten in the morning. In the afternoon, if you are not too tired, you will address the Tibetan government-in-exile and staff at two? The Tibetan Institute of Performing Arts has arranged a special performance for you tomorrow night. After this the Welfare Office would like to take you out to dinner. Your audience with His Holiness has been scheduled for the day after tomorrow at 9:00 A.M. After that the monks at His Holiness's monastery would be most grateful if you could also talk with them. All Tibetans are very happy that you two made it out of Tibet and came here to tell us what you have seen."

Before leaving the Information Office, Thubten loaded our arms with books about Tibet's religion, culture, medicine, struggle, and reconstruction, the XIV Dalai Lama, and dialectics in Buddhist education. "It is the least we can do," he said.

"Do you have *Seven Rivers and Six Ranges?*" John asked.

Thubten rummaged through a cabinet crammed with papers and books and produced two copies of the cherished memoirs of a Khampa resistance fighter.

"I have been trying to find this book for years," John said.

* * *

That evening as the sun melted into the Indian plains, we had drinks with Tenzin Choegyal, His Holiness's youngest brother, on the porch of the Kashmiri Cottage Guest House. "As you can see, I'm the bad sheep of the family!" Tenzin said, introducing himself with a tray of Indian XXX brandy and cold bottled beer. Tenzin's wild laugh put me at ease. Sitting on the patio overlooking the scorched plains, Tenzin said, "Now tell me what *really* happened during the demonstrations."

John extricated a handful of bullet casings from his pocket and asked Tenzin if he could identify them. "Seven and nine millimeter automatic pistols," Tenzin said. "The large one's from an AK-47. Where did you get these?"

"On the rooftop of the police station," John said. "I paid children one yuan for each casing they would bring me. You can have these if you want. I have a whole pocketful."

I started telling Tenzin about the carnage. He jumped up when an American man appeared on the porch. "You rascal," Tenzin said, pinching Avedon affectionately. "Did you meet anyone in the hills? A young woman?" Tenzin introduced us to John Avedon, the author of *In Exile from the Land of Snows.* Avedon was in Dharamsala for a week-long symposium on the brain with five Western scientists and His Holiness. He was full of energy, and playfully tried to pinch Tenzin back.

"Tibet is finally getting some attention from the U.S. Congress," Avedon said. "I testified at a Senate hearing in Washington last week on human rights violations in Tibet. At last Tibet is getting looked at; since Nixon and Kissinger opened relations with China in 1972, Tibet has been aggressively ignored."

"If your CIA hadn't stopped economic and military assistance to the Tibetan freedom fighters," Tenzin said, "Tibet might be a free country today."

"How was your testimony received?" John asked.

"They grilled me because I haven't been there," Avedon said. "China is about to undergo a massive industrialization. The Chinese market has overwhelming appeal to international business. That's what Tibet is up against."

"We better get this over with," I said. John rolled his eyes and I continued, "I threw rocks at the police during the riot."

"They are freedom fighters!" Tenzin exclaimed delightedly. "How many rocks?"

"Several," I admitted, explaining my rage reaction.

"A toast to the freedom fighters!" Tenzin said. "I wish I were your age. I'd love to go to Tibet again." Tenzin was so good-natured and easy to talk to that I felt comfortable asking him why so many Tibetans were named Tenzin. "You see," Tenzin said without any mischief in his face. "My older brother's name is Tenzin Gyatso. So naturally every Tibetan child who is taken to His Holiness is named Tenzin." He laughed again and did his best to pinch Avedon.

"What if Congress finds out about Blake's rock throwing?" John asked. "It will bolster the Chinese charge of foreign instigation."

"You shouldn't have anything to worry about," Avedon said. "You have great reputations: the American physician and lawyer who were arrested in Lhasa for helping the Tibetans."

"What if they ask direct questions?" John asked.

"Whatever you do," Avedon said, "don't ever lie to a congressional hearing, and don't let anyone fluster you, even if they harp on one point. Just stick to your personal experience and explain why you did what you did."

Tenzin successfully pinched Avedon, which ignited cackles of laughter from both of them. Avedon continued, "The State Department has just released a report assessing the status of all minority peoples in China. Ninety percent of the report is on Tibet. The irony here is amazing. The report was published on October 1, the same day as the riot. It states that the Chinese are improving the human rights of the Tibetans.

"You can imagine how embarrassed the State Department was to read that the largest anti-government rioting since 1959 coincided with the publication of their report. The report puts the Chinese population in the Tibet Autonomous Region at 70,000. They also laud the wealth of economic and social improvements.

"The question that interests me now is what effect all this publicity will have on China. Tibet has gotten more media attention in the last two weeks than since the PLA invaded in 1959. Tibet is a thorn in the Chinese side. Tibet represents the threat of a civil and human rights movement in China. But it remains to be seen whether any of this media attention will budge China."

• • •

I was afraid to go into the Tibetan Children's Village auditorium, packed with 800 students, and then have to describe to them the atrocities we had seen. At the Delhi press conference we had eluded the reporters' accusations of throwing rocks. I would have no defense against the acumen and brutal honesty of these children.

Two young boys kicked a clay ball wrapped in plastic with a feather top. John and I made a circle and other children joined in. The children kicked the ball expertly several times from one foot to the other before passing it to the next person. Soon more than fifty children crowded around our circle of hackers. An adult yelled for us to get inside.

Two hundred teachers sat in chairs. Six hundred students sat cross-legged on the floor. Everyone turned to stare as we walked from the back of the hall to a table on the stage. After a brief introduction by the school principal we were left alone with an older student who would translate. Unlike the press conference, we made it through our prepared statements before questions. I said that I had a favorable impression of China and the Chinese people until we got to Tibet. Before discussing the riot I apologized for having to describe horrible things and said that it was important for students to know what was really happening in Tibet, even if it was bad. John covered our arrest, how there was little freedom in the monasteries or schools, and the demonstrations.

"These are the biggest health problems in Tibet," I said, raising bullet casings. Sixteen hundred silent, watery eyes stared back. Many of the children cried during our talk, before their questions were written on scraps of paper and passed to the front of the room. They were questions only children could ask: Do the Tibetans in Tibet hate the Chinese? Will Tibet ever be free again? What happens to our Tibetan brothers and sisters who are taken to prison?

After two hours the jeep whisked us to another hall, where 300 men and women in the Tibetan government-in-exile and staff waited. I had managed to hold back tears in front of the children. Large drops tumbled down my cheeks and splashed on the table as I described the ten-year-old boy who had been shot during the riot. The children were more interested in the current conditions in a Tibet they had never seen. The Tibetan government and staff focused on Tibet's future and the possibility for a free country. For the second time that day we talked and answered questions for two hours.

* * *

I felt numb as we were driven on the narrow ribbon of asphalt to the Tibetan Institute of Performing Arts. We were ushered in next to four Mongolian abbots in the front row. I fell asleep on one of the abbot's shoulders as the M.C. talked about Genghis Khan encountering the Tibetan army in the sixteenth century. Instead of fighting the Tibetans, Genghis Khan adopted Tibetan Buddhism as the state religion. Contemporary Chinese scholars draw on Tibet's succession of military control from Tibet to Mongolia as prima facie evidence that Tibet was part of China; they fail to mention that the same reasoning can be used to show that China was equally a part of Mongolia.

Loud music and acrobatic folk dancing suddenly woke me up, to the abbot's mirth. The dancers slapped their feet loudly and somersaulted across the stage in whirls of color. The men danced and sang and played their guitars for the amusement of the women, who were alternately seductive and independent. Their operatic rendition of nomad life among the spirited yaks left me exhilarated as we stepped out under the stars.

"The Welfare Office wants to take you to dinner at your hotel," Thubten reminded us after the show. For the first time in my life I understood how someone could be killed with kindness. We couldn't refuse. Every Tibetan we met was desperate for news of the their homeland. "The Chinese will do anything to keep information from coming out of Tibet," Thubten explained.

The members of the Welfare Office were waiting to ask the same round of questions we had already answered in detail twice that day. At least, I thought, we were getting practice speaking in public. After dinner we met a stooped Tibetan man who had been waiting in the hall. He unrolled white *khatas* to drape around our shoulders. Tears streamed down his face. Thubten translated, "This man spent twenty years in a Chinese prison. He heard you speak this morning at TCV. He wants to thank you for telling people what is really happening in Tibet. He hopes you will continue to tell the people in your own country."

"It will be our privilege," I said, for the first time realizing our responsibility to speak out against the Chinese disinformation campaign. My training as a physician had prepared me to document the atrocities; traveling in Tibet introduced me to the collective ills of a people.

• • •

We decided to call the Dalai Lama "Your Holiness," the standard greeting. I caught myself holding my breath as the jeep took us to his residence. John tapped his fingertips on his knees, a sure sign of nervousness.

A towering Gurkha soldier with an antiquated rifle and fixed bayonet stood at attention beneath a rounded arch. His piercing gaze sent chills down my spine as we were led to a waiting room where an enormous Hindu couple sat on a bench. A man in a suit recorded our full names, addresses, and passport numbers, after which we were escorted

up a hill to a second waiting room filled with Tibetan artifacts in glass
cases.

"We had an audience with His Holiness last year," the man said,
showing us a picture of them standing next to the Dalai Lama. "I am
not saying we are Buddhists. We are Hindus. But His Holiness is a living God! And the blessing of any God, whether he be Hindu or Moslem
or Buddhist, can only help in the next life." I hoped that this pair would
not accompany us during our precious minutes with His Holiness.

Tenzin Geyche, His Holiness's personal secretary, escorted the
Hindu couple out of the room. John tapped his fingers. I stared at a
thanka. Time slowed to a standstill. I was too nervous to talk when
Geyche returned with the beaming Hindu couple. He led us up the
path to a porch where His Holiness stood in the door. The Dalai Lama
was much taller than I expected. He wore maroon and yellow robes.

"Welcome, my friends," His Holiness said, looking each of us in the
eye. We unrolled our *khatas* awkwardly into his outstretched arms. He
laughed and returned a firm handshake. We were seated next to him on
a couch beneath a topographical map of Tibet that filled the wall.
Sunlight warmed the dragons depicted on the Tibetan rugs and *thankas*
decorating the room. Geyche sat across from us.

"On behalf of six million Tibetans," His Holiness said, "I want to
express my gratitude to both of you. As a human being who very much
believes in truth as a human value, I also want to express my deep
thanks. When tourists saw the true situation, their hearts went toward
the Tibetan side. This really gives us some kind of inspiration and
courage."

"Do you mind if I use a tape recorder?" Geyche asked. "There are so
many things we must ask you."

"One thing," His Holiness said. "During the event that took place in
Lhasa, how many Tibetans came from eastern Kham and Amdo?"

"We couldn't tell," John said. "The Khampas cut off their red tassels."

His Holiness's deep, jolly laugh was infectious. We couldn't help
laughing when he asked us how we had come to Tibet, and John said
that we had hiked to 22,000 feet on Chomolungma in sneakers. We
chatted for fifteen minutes before His Holiness asked again about the
demonstrations.

"Did any Tibetans fire guns?" His Holiness asked. John said that a Tibetan child picked up a machine gun after a Chinese policeman was hit on the head with a rock. The gun was passed over several Tibetans' heads, then smashed on the street. His Holiness was intent on learning the individual details of each man, woman, monk, and child who had died, the numbers of Tibetans and Westerners at each demonstration, and whether the police had shot deliberately.

"You see," His Holiness began, "reporters are asking for news. From Delhi, we hear some whispers that something happened in Lhasa. The radio explained little bits. Actually, you see, we also were taken by surprise." He showed us a photograph of a few monks carrying a Tibetan national flag. "The people around them are looking passive," he said, describing the picture. "So besides the monks, were the Lhasa people fully . . ."

"Involved?" I interjected.

"That's it," His Holiness said. "Were the Lhasa people fully involved?" John gave me a look I hadn't seen since our interrogation by the police. I couldn't help interrupting. We had no idea how much time we would have to speak with the Dalai Lama.

John said that there were approximately a thousand travelers and tourists in Lhasa, and several times that many Tibetans during the October 1 riot. "Dozens of Westerners actually witnessed the event. When the Chinese refused to treat wounded Tibetans, Blake snuck out to treat them. I worked with twenty other foreigners who gathered information for the press," he added.

We identified the picture His Holiness had shown us as having been taken during the September 27 demonstration. "On October 1, the people were ready," John said. "The mistake the Chinese made was to put the monks in the PSB right next to the Jokhang. That became a focus for the crowd's anger. It wasn't a riot in that there was undirected anger. The violence was very much directed at the station in the hope of freeing the monks. And that's exactly what happened. The monks were able to escape."

"Some," I interrupted, and mentioned the three monks who had been shot while trying to escape.

His Holiness asked how many Tibetans were involved with the Chinese police, and if the Tibetan policemen fired on Tibetans. He was particularly interested in people's reactions to Tibetans who worked with the Chinese police. John said that no one had seen a Tibetan policeman fire a weapon, and that initially the Chinese police appeared to fire warning shots over people's heads.

"How many bullets?" His Holiness asked.

"Thousands," I said. "The police fired machine guns and automatic pistols for several hours."

John pulled out his handful of bullet casings and gave some to His Holiness. His Holiness felt the weight of the AK-47 casing in his hands. "I have never seen bullets like these. How did you get them?"

"I paid children one yuan for each one they would bring me from the rooftops of the buildings," John said.

Once again, His Holiness's laughter caught me off guard. "You see," he said, marveling at the size of the AK-47 casing, "some people bring me flowers. You bring me bullets . . . Is it true that monks threw rocks at the police?" I looked at the tape recorder nervously. "Would you feel more comfortable if we turned the tape recorder off?"

"Yes," I said.

"I think people were mostly throwing rocks at the burning police station," John said, giving me a look.

"After seeing several people killed from bullets," I said, unable to contain myself any longer, "and one boy beaten to death by the police, I threw rocks at the police. I didn't know what else to do to stop the police from shooting unarmed people. I was so angry I wanted to kill. This still bothers me very much."

"You must not hate the Chinese for what they are doing," His Holiness said. "The Chinese are wonderful people. It is their government that makes trouble."

"How do you feel about monks throwing rocks?" John asked.

"You see," His Holiness said. "Buddhism is a religion that respects all life on the planet. We try not to even slap mosquitoes, but we don't always succeed. Just because a monk takes vows and wears robes does not mean that he stops being human. For a monk to throw a rock at a policeman is very sad. But I understand how throwing rocks could be a natural response to an extreme situation. Tibetans have been living under very sad conditions for more than forty years.

"The Chinese are very good at preventing information from leaking out of Tibet," His Holiness continued after a long pause. "Even if I had known what happened during the demonstrations, there are so many constraints on what I can say. The Indian government has been very generous to the Tibetan people, but still I am not free to make any political . . ." His Holiness looked again to Geyche for help with word choice.

"Statements?" I interjected. John kicked me under the table.

"Yes, that's it. It is the same in every country I visit. I am always told not to make any political statements. It is a difficult position. What am I to do?" His Holiness smiled benevolently.

John said, "When we were arrested we found out a little of what Tibetans go through when they are arrested. The Chinese tried to get us to denounce you and say that Tibet had always been a part of China."

"The monks are tortured in prison," I said, and described the monks who had bones broken in prison and were refused medical treatment, and that at least one monk had died from beatings during and after the riot. "The monks are especially afraid of lethal injections."

"We must always be thinking of solutions," His Holiness said. "For some time now I have had this idea of, how should I call it . . . Buddho-communism. You see, Buddhism and communism have many things in common. If the conditions of my people are ever going to improve, there must be some compromise. This compromise is Buddho-communism."

"Do congressional resolutions put pressure on China to stop human rights abuses?" John asked.

"Everything helps. Tibet is getting more publicity now than ever before. So far China has not changed."

"We should boycott goods made in China," I said. "As long as the State Department is primarily interested in big business, we have to organize grass roots organizations."

His Holiness looked at me quizzically. "Even in your State Department you will find people who are sympathetic with oppressed people all around the world."

"Blake generalizes easily," John said.

"One of the great things Tibetan Buddhism has to offer to this world is the Bodhisattva ideal," His Holiness said. "In Tibetan Buddhism, we do not believe in gods. We believe that perfection is possible in this lifetime. Ever since Sakyamuni, Bodhisattvas have shown that it is possible to reach enlightenment." His Holiness laughed again and I felt lighter. "This is lucky for me. You see, with so many things to do for my people, I have not had time to keep up with my meditations."

Sensing that our audience was about to end, John asked, "Is it true that West Germany and Switzerland are negotiating with China to dump nuclear waste in Tibet?"

"I have read something to this effect in the Western press," His Holiness said, and continued to discuss his concern that nuclear waste on the Tibetan Plateau could pollute all of Asia's great rivers. I didn't interrupt him when he occasionally paused to search for a word. This surprised John.

"Do you have any difficulty answering the press?" His Holiness asked suddenly. He looked worried. John said that the historical record was clearly in Tibet's favor. I was pleased that the Dalai Lama sought our advice, even if we could not answer his last question: "Do you know anyone close to Ronald Reagan who is a good human being?"

CHAPTER ELEVEN

DHARMA AND THE RED MEN

A FTER RETURNING HOME, I did not need another physician to diagnose that I had a mild case of post-traumatic stress disorder. I cried when I described the explicit violence I had witnessed in Tibet to my family and friends. Loud noises made me duck as though I were under fire. I continued to wake up crying in the night. With patience and help from my family—and with regaining the thirty pounds I had lost—I began to recover. More than anything, writing about my experiences helped me to cope.

My mother waited for several days after my return, until I had begun to settle down, before telling me what had happened to her during the turbulence. The initial press reports out of Tibet said that we had been arrested, and that an angry mob had burned the police station to the ground. "For ten days I thought you were dead," she sobbed. "I didn't dare leave the house in case I missed a call with news of your whereabouts." My mother explained that while the unrest had raged the phone rang day and night. She took forty pages of notes on a legal pad from her conversations with parliamentarians, government agencies, and concerned people around the world, which included many requests for press interviews and speaking engagements at universities and human rights organizations.

● ● ●

John and I had a week at home to recuperate before undergoing a live interview for CNN. Bernard Shaw introduced us as "eyewitnesses" in

Tibet and asked what the Dalai Lama's reaction had been. John said the Dalai Lama was a nonviolent man and was sorry for the deaths. I began explaining the escalation of events, from the Dalai Lama's proposing his Five-Point Peace Plan to—

"We couldn't get any reports," Shaw interrupted. "Why did you subject yourself to that kind of physical jeopardy?"

"There were no reporters in Lhasa," John said. "This was an historic moment for Tibet. We felt we needed to take pictures and document what was happening, and to get those reports out to the West."

"What did you see?" Shaw asked. "What did you hear? What did you feel?"

John said that he watched a group of Tibetans overturn a jeep and light it on fire, and that he couldn't believe this was happening.

"What were you doing physically?"

"I was in the Tibetan crowd," John said. "Taking pictures, trying to stay undercover between streetlight posts and tables. Tibetans kept begging us to take pictures and show them to the Dalai Lama."

"One effect of this is you sometimes wake up crying?"

"That was me," I said, angered by the question. I held up the bullet casings and said that twelve people had died.

"Were you aiding the victims?"

"Definitely," I said. "I tried to stop profuse bleeding. Most of the time I could only document how someone had died."

"Based on what you saw, what do you make of the situation in Lhasa, in Tibet, as it relates to the Chinese and the policies affecting the Tibetans?"

"Tibetans have been living under Chinese military occupation for thirty-seven years," I said, talking as fast as I could. "China is committing genocide in Tibet. Colonization is the biggest threat to Tibetan autonomy." I knew I had only seconds left, and suddenly recalled the woman who was sterilized after the nurse gave her newborn a lethal injection.

● ● ●

The next day we addressed the Congressional Human Rights Caucus, co-founded by Tom Lantos (D-CA) and John Porter (R-IL) to make human rights concerns a bigger part of U.S. foreign policy. Lantos spoke eloquently of his own experience with Nazi Germany's attempt to exterminate the Jews, and said that Tibet was another holocaust. Charlie Rose (D-NC), a large, impressive gentleman, said in a Southern drawl that China's occupation of Tibet sickened him. He gave his full support to the cause of Tibetan independence.

"Before I went to Tibet," I said, "I expected Tibet's biggest health hazards to be intestinal . . . I lost thirty pounds while consuming mostly yak byproducts." People laughed and continued eating. "But I learned that these are the biggest health hazards in Tibet," I said, raising the bullet casings. People stopped eating as I described the killing and the wounded Tibetans who feared imprisonment if they went to a Chinese hospital.

John spoke in terms of human and civil rights. His words sounded removed from our experiences, but the congressmen paid attention to phrases like "restrictions on freedom to practice religion" and "arrest and imprisonment without due process." He mentioned that the Tibetans' living conditions were substandard compared to those of Chinese immigrants who received higher wages and better jobs, that Chinese was the language of commerce and industry, and that massive population transfer was conspicuous in Lhasa.

As at the New Delhi press conference, we were treated to a sumptuous feast and assured that we had done well. We met representatives from Amnesty International and Asia Watch and reporters for the *Christian Science Monitor*, the *Washington Times*, the *Washington Post*, and the *American Medical News*.

*　*　*

I felt puny standing in the State Department's marble lobby of skyscraping columns and country flags. We had requested a meeting with Bart Flaherty, the head of the "China Desk," in order to discuss the Tibet section of the department's annual "country report." Flaherty listened politely while John showed slides of the escalating violence: the police beating monks, Tibetans burning the police station, the ten-year-old boy shot through the chest who died in my hands, Champa Tenzin coming out of the burning police station with third-degree burns. Flaherty squirmed.

"What is the department's position on the demonstration?" John asked.

"The State Department recognizes that the People's Republic of China perpetrates a number of human rights violations throughout China," Flaherty said. "We also believe that Tibet is an internal affair of China's."

John looked stunned. It was as though we were talking to Mr. Chen, our Chinese jailer. Unable to conceal my anger, I shouted, "What about people being slaughtered?"

Flaherty became red-faced and pushed his chair back. "The State Department is expressing its concern through the appropriate diplomatic channels."

John opened the State Department's country report on China, which was dated October 1, the same day as the riot. In reference to the assessment that the Tibetan Autonomous Region had 30,000 Chinese immigrants, John estimated that Lhasa alone had at least 70,000 Chinese, more than the number of Tibetans. He showed a panoramic photo he had taken from the Potala's rooftop of the newly constructed cinderblock buildings in the valley.

"You can't determine population from a few photographs," Flaherty said.

"Tibetans are being tortured in prisons as we speak," I shouted. Flaherty moved his chair back.

"Did you see anyone being tortured?" he asked. I said that I had met monks beaten with cattle prods during interrogation.

John pressed Flaherty to justify the State Department's reversal on Tibet as of 1972, when the U.S. China policy changed. "It's pure politics—it's not based on historical realities or what's right or wrong," John charged. He supported his points with slides and a calm demeanor, while I tried to argued with Flaherty, who kept moving his chair back. After three hours, Flaherty had moved his chair to the wall and could retreat no farther.

At one point another man came into the room and said, "It looks like there's going to be a demonstration in Ithaca tomorrow. The Chinese ambassador is visiting Cornell University." I did not mention that Ithaca was my home town, or that I had accepted an invitation to speak at the demonstration. They would find out soon enough.

"It's genocide," I said, exasperated. Flaherty repeated that the State Department considered Tibet an internal affair of China's.

"The U.S. could stop selling arms to China that are used against the Tibetans," John said.

"We should boycott goods made in China," I said.

"I'm going to be frank," Flaherty said. "The State Department empathizes with the plight of the Tibetans. We recognize that China is committing human rights violations throughout mainland China and Tibet. However, it is the department's position that Tibet is an internal affair of China's."

PART THREE
RETURN TO TIBET

CHAPTER TWELVE

WHY ARE THEY LAUGHING?

L HASA'S INDEPENDENCE DEMONSTRATIONS in the fall of 1987 alerted the world to Tibetan nationalism. China promptly responded by closing Tibet to reporters, parliamentarians, and international human rights organizations. A trickle of overland travelers brought out stories of brutal torture and repression, and of continued demonstrations occurring throughout the country. Although the world press reported the Chinese atrocities in "Shangri-La," their interest in Tibet's plight was fleeting. Even more distressing was the Reagan/Bush Administration's tolerance of Chinese oppression.

What John and I had witnessed in Lhasa changed our lives. John went to work for the International Campaign for Tibet in Washington. I postponed my residency to write a narrative account of our trip. Two years went by quickly. Devoting ourselves full-time to advocacy work, we wrote a dozen articles for magazines and newspapers. We presented testimony to several congressional committees and the German parliament, and gave fifty talks to university and human rights groups in North America. To help foster new Tibet support groups after our talks, we developed a pamphlet with useful information for fledgling activists on fundraising, literature tables, sample letters to elected representatives, and civil disobedience.

At times, both of us wondered if our memories of the explicit violence that we had witnessed in Lhasa were becoming exaggerated, and if the violence implicit in the daily lives of the Tibetans had subsided. If the Tibetans continued to live under extreme repression, we felt that we owed it to ourselves and to the Tibetans to document these conditions to the best of our professional abilities.

In the fall of 1988, John and I traveled separately to India to interview Tibetan refugees. We had developed a questionnaire to investigate prison conditions and China's family-planning policy in Tibet, and hoped to write a report if we gathered enough information. I also wanted to know more about Tibetan medicine. I already had established a written correspondence with Namhla Takla, the director of the *Mendzekhang* in Dharamsala. Now I would have the chance to speak with her in person.

◆ ◆ ◆

Mrs. Takla's office at the *Mendzekhang* looked out over forested mountains that rolled onto the arid Indian subcontinent. Mrs. Takla served tea and explained the major problems facing the *Mendzekhang*. First, there was a lack of money. Second, they did not have the facilities to make enough medicine. Third, they had a difficult time getting the necessary herbs; the Chinese had pressured the Nepalese to forbid all exports of herbs.

"Musk comes from Tibet," Mrs. Takla explained. "The Chinese are taking all the musk that enters Nepal for themselves."

Mrs. Takla also said that Tibetans in exile needed to train more *menlops* (Tibetan medical students). They were currently building accommodations for visiting scientists, doctors, and medical students. "The older doctors are very traditional and stubborn," she said. "I often have to side with the younger doctors, which makes trouble for me."

Mrs. Takla smiled broadly as Dr. Choedak stepped into the room. This was the Dalai Lama's personal physician, a slightly stooped man in his sixties. "His ears must be ringing," Mrs. Takla said to me. She explained to Dr. Choedak in Tibetan that I had treated wounded in Lhasa. Dr. Choedak held my hands as he talked. Mrs. Takla translated the information that Tibetans had excellent medicines for asthma, hypertension, adult-onset diabetes, arthritis, cancer, and multiple sclerosis.

Dr. Choedak was equally forthright about the shortcomings of Tibetan medicine. Newly trained Tibetan doctors didn't focus as much on diet and behavior. Even before 1959, there was less focus on meditating, massage, and medicine baths. These things needed to be revised. Western and Tibetan doctors should do research together and take the best from both systems.

"All of this depends on training the young *menlops*," Mrs. Takla said. "Most of our medical students learn to speak English at the Children's Village, but they do not know the Western medical terms. Dr. Choedak would be honored if you would stay here with us, and give a series of lectures on Western medicine to the students while you are here."

Dr. Choedak took me to my room. It had the simplicity of a monk's quarters, with bare walls, a bed, and a desk. I sat down to begin outlining my first lecture and he returned in a few minutes with Lobsang, a young monk who had just arrived from Lhasa. Neither Dr. Choedak nor Lobsang could speak English, and my Tibetan was still restricted to the social amenities. I drew a crude map of the world in my journal with the U.S. and Tibet prominently featured. I asked Lobsang how he left Tibet and he answered "Yes," as he did to all subsequent inquiries. Although it was frustrating not being able to communicate, I was struck by how forcefully he spoke. Half an hour and many cups of butter tea later, I realized that I needed a translator.

●　●　●

At Dharamsala's Office of Information I met Norbu, a Tibetan who had grown up in Switzerland. Norbu was the most staid Tibetan I had ever met, and spoke English with a Swiss-German accent. He agreed to translate during my three-week stay, during which I would be interviewing Tibetan refugees. On our way to have tea we met Kelsang, the Jokhang scribe I had treated the previous year. He was taller than I remembered. He also had sixteen stubbleless scars on his shaved head.

Kelsang was brimming with details of the special torture teams that came to Lhasa in the fall of 1987. Individuals were first stripped and beaten. The torturers screamed, "Tibet's freedom will be your food," as they crushed one man's testicles; another man died from being beaten with a bayonet. Hearing about these victims of torture brought back a flood of horrific memories. I wanted desperately to leave, even before I'd started the work I'd come for, but struggled to record all of the details.

"Kelsang was inside the Jokhang Temple during the March 5, 1988, demonstration," Norbu translated. "At 11:00 A.M., 700 Chinese police stormed the monastery. They used ladders to climb the walls. Nine hundred Tibetans were sheltered inside, including a hundred women and children. Another thousand Tibetans stood outside the main door. The police used tear gas and beat everyone with clubs. Many people were bleeding. Nine people died in the first hour. Kelsang does not know how many died in prison afterward. Sixty-four people were taken to prison. Tibetans attacked a Chinese policeman taking photographs from the roof. They hit him on the head with stones and threw him down onto the street. He died in the ambulance on the way to the People's Hospital.

"Kelsang was bleeding profusely from wounds all over his body," Norbu continued, speaking without emotion. "He went to the *Mendzekhang* in an ambulance, and spent two months there. The police came in every day to interrogate and photograph the wounded. They wanted to take Kelsang to prison but the doctors complained that Kelsang was too ill to move. Then the doctors discharged him secretly. When he went back to the Jokhang the Chinese police tried to capture him and he escaped."

Besides the scars on his scalp and the rest of his body, Kelsang still had headaches and had not regained his previous energy level, but he smiled as he told me this and posed for pictures. "He has a message from Champa Tenzin," Norbu said. "Champa Tenzin was in the *Mendzekhang* for one month, then the police kept him in Sangyip Prison for four months, but he is alive. He sends his regards."

* * *

I heard many eyewitness accounts of other demonstrations throughout Tibet. Twenty-nine nuns from the Shongsey and Garu nunneries were arrested for demonstrating outside the Jokhang on March 4, 1988. The next day fifty-three monks from Ganden Monastery started another demonstration that resulted in the police using tear gas and bullets to break up the crowd. Although the estimates of deaths and arrests varied, it appeared that the police used increasing force to quell each successive uprising. I also found the individual Tibetans I interviewed to be credible.

Individual descriptions of torture at Lhasa's Gutsa, Sangyip, Titchu, Utitod, and Drapchi prisons were remarkably similar. The prisoners were beaten while their captors forced them to denounce the Dalai Lama and Tibetan independence. Women were raped with cattle prods at several facilities. The most severe treatment involved attack dogs ripping flesh from prisoners' legs and genitals.

I struggled through each interview. One man who had fought in the resistance told me that he had seen Chinese soldiers kill his wife and three children. He fought in Tibet until 1959 and left with the Dalai Lama. He became bored with life in exile and enlisted in a special regiment of Tibetans in the Indian army who were known for their endurance and determination.

"The Indians lost six battalions trying to free Bangladesh," the man said. "The Gurkhas also failed. Our commander told our regiment that the Chinese were in the swamps. We waded through those swamps with our rifles over our heads. In a month we liberated Bangladesh."

* * *

Dr. Dorje Gyalpo took me to give my first lecture to the *menlops* the following morning. I knew that Tibetan medicine had a detailed knowledge of fetal development, and I had outlined a lecture on human embryology. At first my room at the college had seemed very comfortable, but something biting my ankles had prevented me from sleeping. I slapped but heard nothing. Something bit my neck. Again I slapped, but no culprits could be found. This biting and slapping continued until dawn.

That morning I faced sixty Tibetan medical students sitting upright at their desks with the sort of undivided attention I had never seen in U.S. schools. Dr. Gyalpo sat in the front row with Mrs. Takla and Dr. Namgyal, the head of the pharmacy. "The Buddha taught that a questioning mind is a lifelong endeavor," Dr. Gyalpo said in concluding his introduction to my talk, asking the students to save their questions for the end.

I began with an evolutionary perspective: "One billion lifetimes ago, one-celled organisms formed in the oceans. As these organisms became more complex they developed specialized organs for things like eating, locomotion, and reproduction. After millions of years amphibious beings crawled onto land." I drew pictures to illustrate the phylogenetic explosion of plant and animal species, including dinosaurs, on the chalkboard. This thoroughly confused and interested everyone. "All of the animals on the planet have much more in common than we might think, and all come from the union of cells," I said.

Dr. Gyalpo excitedly handed me a box of multi-colored chalk. "Where do babies come from?" he asked. The *menlops* laughed nervously. Dr. Gyalpo listened politely to my answer that human beings came from the union of the father's sperm and the mother's egg. The students talked while I drew egg and sperm cells and said that the fertilized egg evolved through amphibious and mammalian stages before it developed into human form.

"What is the nature of the developing fetal conscience?" Dr. Gyalpo asked.

"How are they joined?" Mrs. Takla asked.

"Why is it dangerous for a pregnant woman to take an X-ray?" Dr. Namgyal asked.

I answered each question to the best of my knowledge, which led to more questions. It was decided that I would give a lecture every other day. My one-hour lectures to the *menlops* evolved into a dependable three hours; no matter what I started talking about, the students inevitably asked two hours of questions. Most of the males asked about sex. Many passed me notes: "If I do whole night intercourse, about five to six times, is it possible to recover sperms on that particular night?" "In Tibetan medicine, food is the essence of sperm. Is it the same in Western medicine?" "If someone licks sperm, is it good for the body? (DON'T ASK WHO HAS ASKED THIS QUESTION)" "What is the difference between 1) taking sperm purposefully *without* a partner 2) sperm coming while having sex *with* a partner? I have heard that the first one is not good, whereas in the second case the male gets some nutrient from the female."

One man, Dokpa, looked like a beatnik astrology student with his crew cut and goatee. He asked the most difficult questions, such as, "What are the merits and demerits of the Tibetan and Western medical systems? Please state them honestly." I replied that both systems had excellent pharmacopoeias. I added that because Western doctors relied heavily on technology, they relied less on their clinical skills to diagnose an illness. Dokpa also offered his own intriguing insights. During a talk on the central nervous system he likened the function of the brain to a bird on a tree. "When the tree falls," he said, "the bird flies away."

"Exactly what is adrenaline?" Dokpa asked in the middle of my explaining about our endocrine glands. "How can we know its effects?" I could not resist whispering, "Do you want to know what adrenaline does?"

"Please tell us," I heard Dokpa say. I waited for the *menlops* to lean forward and become silent. Then I screamed. The *menlops* jumped back in terror, knocking over chairs and tables. Fortunately, no one was hurt. For once I, who often seemed to strike them as an inexhaustible source of amusement, was able to laugh at them.

* * *

I spoke with a Tibetan nurse named Chimi who had worked for three years at Lhasa's People's Hospital. She explained to me China's family-planning policy for urban Tibetans. Chimi had learned English well and we were able to speak without a translator.

"Tibetan women are allowed to have two children," Chimi said, "but if they have one this is considered best. The work unit leader is in charge of enforcing the central government's policies. In public meetings that everyone is required to attend, women are told that it is best to have one child. If they are sterilized after the first child, praise will be given for being a good citizen.

"If a woman has a second child," she continued, "the child will have rights. But this is discouraged. Sterilization is done automatically on many women delivering their second child at Chinese hospitals.

"Having a third child is strongly discouraged. An illegal child has no ration card for the monthly allotment of Tibetan dietary staples at government stores: seven kilos of *tsampa*, one-half kilo yak butter, and cooking oil. Without a ration card a child cannot go to school, do organized work, travel, or own property.

"In villages there are thousands of illegal children. Tibetans would rather have their own way." When asked how these children survived, Chimi said that such "illegal persons" had to do things like collect dung.

"Women also are fined for having a third or fourth child," Chimi said. When asked if she could list individuals' names, Chimi said that she did not know any women in Lhasa who had more than two children. Since 1983, there had been a new policy that all women living near Chinese hospitals had to deliver their babies in the hospital birth-control units.

When asked if there were differences in the way Chinese and Tibetan patients were treated, Chimi first said that Tibetan and Chinese women were treated equally. Then, in her next sentence, she outlined two systems of health care: "There are two sections in the hospital: one for government officials and people with good jobs, another for ordinary people. The difference is better food and a cleaner environment. Most Tibetan women have babies at home. The Chinese officials and their friends always get the best food, the best medicines, and the best care. The Chinese also have the best jobs and look down on the Tibetans, who have menial jobs, smell, and are not clean."

My stomach felt queasy as Chimi described how "unauthorized" pregnancies were routinely terminated with lethal injections. Chimi said that she herself had given hundreds of these injections.

"There must be *some* improvements in health care since the Chinese came?" I asked her.

Chimi shook her head. "The Chinese brought tuberculosis, for which Tibetans have no natural resistance and Tibetan medicine has no cure. Unemployment and alcoholism are also higher, especially among young Tibetans. Infant mortality is one in six babies, one of the highest in the world. Life expectancy for a Tibetan is ten years less than for a Chinese living in Lhasa."

Chimi seemed on the verge of politely excusing herself. I thanked her and asked if she would list women she had seen get abortions or sterilizations at the Lhasa People's Hospital. In less than an hour, Chimi furnished me with a list of the names, ages, dates, procedures, and complications of twelve women who had abortions by D&C during the first trimester; four women given injections to induce abortion during their second and third trimesters; and six women who had been sterilized.

Before leaving, Chimi asked if she could keep the list. She knew of more women but did not have time to write them all down.

Two nights later Chimi handed me three sheets of paper that listed fifty-three women who were sterilized after an abortion. I asked how she could remember so many names and dates from four years ago. She replied that both of her parents were doctors and taught her to have a good memory. I quizzed her on individual details until I was convinced that they were internally consistent. This appeared to insult her.

"Even if a woman is forced to have an abortion," Chimi said, "she will feel guilty for the rest of her life. We are seeing families break up because of this. For these reasons, Tibetans have nicknamed the People's Hospital 'The Butcher's Place.'"

* * *

Unidentified insect bites continued to plague my nights. I could not sleep until I had scratched each bite raw. After ten nights I finally found my first bedbug. It was as large as a raisin and made a splotch on my pillow. A second bedbug clinging to the wall next to my head also made a stain. I soon found dozens of plump, raisin-sized bedbugs clinging to the underside of the bed's wood frame. I dragged the mattress to the far side of my room and slept soundly.

In the morning I told Mrs. Takla my first complete Tibetan sentence: "Nga nangla deshik manpo do" (There are a lot of bedbugs in my room). That afternoon I returned to find all of my possessions, mattress, and bedding airing out in the sun. "The *deshiks* (bedbugs) will not be returning to your room," Mrs. Takla said. "We sprayed everything with DDT."

* * *

Norbu arranged for a Land Rover to take us to the Bir refugee camp, a four-hour drive from Dharamsala. The Tibetans at the camp had come from all parts of Tibet, and most had left their native land within the last year. They would be excellent sources of information, Norbu reasoned. Chimi came along, but she refused to get into the passenger seat. "The doctor must be comfortable," she said and squeezed into the back seat next to Norbu and two other Tibetan travelers. A hefty woman who joined us also refused my offer to share the spacious front seat and squeezed on top of Norbu's lap. Norbu's polite smile belied a strained expression.

"What are you doing?" Norbu shouted as I forced my way into the entanglement of elbows and knees and moans. I said that either someone had to sit in the front seat with me or I would ride with everyone else in the back seat. This was not altogether altruistic; if an accident on a steep mountain road didn't kill me, I would have been crushed by their weight.

"*Amchi-la, neumba*" (crazy doctor), the driver said, and pulled the woman off Norbu's lap to sit in the front seat with us.

British volunteer teachers at Bir welcomed us and passed the word that an American doctor was documenting torture and sterilization. Anyone who had something to say about this should come to the meeting house. Young Tibetans started lining up outside the door. We interviewed refugees sixteen hours a day for two days. An average interview took two hours. Most provided me with hard first-hand information.

For an hour one young nun named Dechen would talk only about her nun friend who was taken to Drapchi Prison for participating in the October 1 demonstration. "Tamdy is twenty years old," Dechen said. "I visited her in prison." I interrupted to ask how she had been allowed to visit a prisoner. She said that prisoners were occasionally allowed visits by family and friends.

"Tamdy received daily beatings and torture," Norbu translated. "The police forced Tamdy and eleven other women to run for hours while they beat them with cattle prods. The dogs attacked Tamdy many times. The dogs must have had very sharp teeth because there is one place in her right thigh with a large hunk of flesh missing."

I asked for more details about the torture, and for the names of the police who beat Tamdy. Dechen looked insulted and would not answer questions for a long time. I apologized for asking so many questions, and explained that they were essential for my report.

"After the October 1 demonstration," Norbu said when Dechen began talking, "the police came to Dechen's workplace and took her to the police station. There they produced a thick book that she was told contained all of her crimes. The police never opened the book. She told the police that she had not done anything bad. She was then taken to a different room where they touched her mouth with an electric stick many times. This felt as though her mouth had exploded. She lost consciousness.

"Later Chinese policemen stripped her. She cried as the men ripped her clothes off with the help of women police. She was beaten over her body with the electric stick on her breasts, mouth, and head, and lost consciousness many times. She feels that since this she has had difficulty remembering things and learning new words. She thinks this is from the electric sticks. This lasted three days at Drapchi Prison. The male police were Chinese. The women were Moslems, from Pakistan or Kashmir. They had been living in Lhasa for a long time."

Before being released from Drapchi, Dechen was told not to say anything about what had happened to her in prison. She was also warned that if she ever participated in another demonstration, she would be treated much worse.

• • •

The next day we interviewed Jigme, a Tibetan policeman from Lhasa who said that he had tortured his own people. I began by asking about China's family-planning policy and was surprised to hear him say that it was the birth-control teams, not the police, who were responsible for bringing recalcitrant women to the hospital for abortions and sterilizations.

"As soon as a woman gives birth," he said, "she has to register the baby with the local police. The police say, 'Be careful you don't get pregnant again. If you do, you won't get a ration card for the child.'"

I changed the subject and asked why he became a police officer. Jigme said that he thought police training would teach him to be versatile. He learned how to drive a motorcycle, jeep, and truck, to fire pistols and machine guns, and to detect and interrogate criminals. His face saddened. "If he did not do what he was told, the officers would ostracize him at public meetings. The police are very nationalistic," Norbu said.

Jigme answered questions about his police work. "For political reasons," Norbu translated, "the police have a special unit called the *gowanchu* that arrests suspects and takes them to prison. A separate unit, the *gentsayan*, does interrogation. Most officers in both units are Chinese. In general, the *gentsayan* finds out if the prisoner is involved in the underground or demonstrations. They extract confessions and get prisoners to denounce the Dalai Lama.

"Political prisoners are put in a cold, dark cell," he continued. "Depending on the case, prisoners are chained at the ankles and wrists. They often are kept for more than three months. During Jigme's time they used an electric cattle prod with a battery. If they touch the head for fifteen minutes the person will be unconscious. There is also a special rope to tie the wrists and ankles that becomes tighter if the prisoner moves."

Jigme described how the treatment given to prisoners depended on how they cooperated with the police. His face bore no emotion when Norbu said, "If a prisoner is adamant and says that Tibet is independent, he will be stripped and beaten. If the prisoner dies during the beatings the police are not responsible. It is the prisoner's fault if he dies. The police have the upper hand and are free to beat the prisoners to death."

Jigme also said that he tried to do "good things." He gave food and clothes in secret to the prisoners. Sometimes he was able to warn a family before they came to arrest someone.

"There is a special Chinese doctor for prisons," Norbu said. "If a prisoner is about to die the doctor gives just enough treatment to keep him alive and lengthen the torture. If the prisoner dies easily, he cannot be tortured for long." I asked Jigme if he had seen any torture techniques. Tears streaked his cheeks. He spoke in choked sentence fragments about how he had beaten Tibetan prisoners with electric sticks, hung them by their thumbs and ankles over a heater, suspended them in ice baths, and given injections to make them "*neumba*" (crazy).

I asked about the dogs and Jigme said the *owlies* (attack dogs) were trained to bite prisoners on command. He laughed and said that prisoners told him many things at this time. "The dogs eat better than the soldiers," Norbu translated. "They are allotted 300 yuan a month, more than a Tibetan makes in one year."

Jigme said that the reason he left Tibet was to help the Tibetan cause. He felt that he had to tell the Dalai Lama what he had done. Perhaps this could help his people.

* * *

The most outrageous account came from a monk named Tashi who described a mobile birth-control team that came to his village in Amdo in 1987. "When the barley turned brown," Tashi began, "I watched a mobile birth-control team set up their tent next to my monastery. First the villagers were informed that the team had arrived, and that all women had to report to the tent or there would be grave consequences, like fines of 1,000 yuan to women who did not comply. The team also said that sterilization was part of a world constitution; women all over the world have this done. The women who went peacefully received medical care. Women who resisted were rounded up by the police and taken by force. No medical care was given."

"All pregnant women were taken to the tent for operations," Tashi continued. "Women nine months' pregnant had their babies taken out. I saw many girls crying. I heard their screams as they waited for their turn to go into the tent, and I saw the growing pile of fetuses build outside the tent, which smelled horrible. I saw this in two villages. I arrived in my own village too late. The birth-control team had already been there."

As a physician I believe that a woman has the right to choose if she wants to have an abortion. Such forced abortions and sterilizations were an outrageous breach of human conduct. What Tashi described was a mass sterilization that seemed designed to control the Tibetan population.

"The mobile birth-control teams were initiated in 1982," Tashi continued. "Since 1987 there has been an increase in the number and frequency of the teams that move to remote towns and nomad areas. The mobile birth-control teams do not do abortions and sterilizations on Chinese women. Few Chinese live in these areas. Many Tibetans have been shamed by what has happened. All of the Tibetans in Amdo are talking about this. We are outraged that China is trying to end the Tibetan race. At the same time, we are helpless to prevent it."

* * *

It took John and me one year to get our report of torture in Tibet published. We had wanted to include information about family planning, but we had not gotten enough first-hand accounts of abortion and sterilization. We had recorded eight first-hand accounts of torture. This was not a large enough number to provide a comprehensive accounting of Chinese prisons in Tibet, but it established that Tibetan political prisoners are routinely tortured, a point China had previously denied.

We sent a draft of our report to Physicians for Human Rights, a Boston-based group that had already published reports on human rights abuses in Chile, Czechoslovakia, Iraq, Israel, Kenya, Panama, and the Republic of Korea. After sending the manuscript to their external readers and board of directors, PHR published *The Suppression of a People: Accounts of Torture and Imprisonment in Tibet* in November of 1989.

The Dalai Lama received the Nobel Peace Prize that same month. Suddenly the world press exhibited a new concern for Tibet. The Dalai Lama's extensive travels and speaking around the world increased awareness of the cultural genocide being committed in Tibet. It also made me realize that the torture and imprisonment of Tibetans was generally acknowledged by human rights organizations and the United Nations, as it was by the governments of more than a hundred countries around the world. At the same time these institutions seemed inured to the issue of torture. The issue of forced abortions and sterilizations, which I was determined to explore further, was potentially much more powerful; it was still very poorly documented.

I developed a questionnaire on family planning with help from Rinchen Kandala, the head of the Tibetan Women's Association in Dharamsala. Mrs. Kandala volunteered to find and interview women. Nevertheless, the project had to be postponed for a year. The two years since I had graduated from medical school had slipped away; if I did not do my internship, I would not be able to get my license to practice medicine.

I chose Saint Vincent's Hospital in New York City's Greenwich Village at which to do my internship, because it offered one of the few programs in the country that trained general practitioners with rotations in obstetrics, pediatrics, psychiatry, surgery, internal medicine, radiology, cardiology, intensive care units, and the emergency room. I also liked the nuns who ran the hospital, and appreciated their mission to serve the poor and the indigent.

During my internship I worked a hundred hours a week, with thirty-six-hour shifts every second to fourth night, for one year. Even when I was exhausted I still felt grateful for the times I could get away. I loved staying up all night in the emergency room surrounded by life-saving technology and highly skilled personnel. I learned to appreciate the nuns even more, especially when they let me do an extra month of trauma surgery. Nowhere is Western medicine as intense as it is in the resuscitation of people with multiple trauma. Although I was impressed with our incredible array of medical technology, I never forgot the Tibetans, whose health-care needs were more basic: freedom.

After my internship, I started to work part-time at a walk-in clinic that provided primary care to eastern Long Islanders. I was determined to revise my nonfiction account of traveling to Tibet (which eventually became this book) and to investigate China's family-planning policy in Tibet.

* * *

In December of 1990, the Dalai Lama gave the Kalachakra teachings at Sarnath, Northern India, where the Buddha gave his first sermon after his enlightenment in 600 B.C. The Kalachakra is the initiation into what Tibetan Buddhists call the "path of compassion." Historically, these teachings are given by the Dalai Lama only a few times during the course of his life, usually during periods of great strife. Tenzin Gyatso, the Fourteenth Dalai Lama, has already given more than twenty Kalachakras.

A quarter of a million Tibetans came to Bodh Gaya, the site of the Buddha's enlightenment, when the Dalai Lama gave the teachings there in 1985. In 1990, only 2,000 Tibetans from Tibet managed to evade Chinese border patrols in order to attend. Sarnath, nevertheless, was overwhelmed when more than 100,000 Tibetan refugees arrived from settlements in India and Nepal. For lay Tibetans and monks the Kalachakra was an opportunity to see a living god. For me, it was an opportunity to interview recent arrivals on China's family-planning policy in Tibet.

Traveling overland on a low budget meant that I could not afford to pay a translator. Then I met a boy named Tenzin on the train to Varanasi, the nearest city. He was a shy eighteen-year-old, a recent graduate of the Tibetan Children's Village in Dharamsala, who volunteered his services when he found out that I was going to interview women about China's family planning in Tibet. He turned as red as the betel-nut juice the Indian men spit on the floor when I wrote down a list of relevant medical terms he would need to use. "Personally," Tenzin told me, "I am not knowing the vagina."

Tenzin turned out to be an excellent translator. Because he had grown up in Lhasa, he spoke fluent Tibetan and Chinese. As an exile, he learned English at the Tibetan Children's Village. His mother worked for the Tibetan Women's Association, and she let us sleep outside her temporary office at the monastery in Sarnath.

Tenzin and I went to the new arrivals' camp twice a day for two weeks. Our first visit proved to be a good orientation. We found the reception committee inside the registration tent. Wearing coats and ties, they were easy to distinguish among the horde of new arrivals who were ecstatic to have made it to India. Namgyal, the head of the committee, offered to screen all women for first-hand knowledge of China's family-planning policy. He also led us to a women's tent, where twenty-eight women shied away from us when we entered. Namgyal introduced us to a woman with dozens of well-scratched bites on her face, arms, and bare feet beneath her soiled *chuba*. He announced that it was her duty to tell us if she had ever experienced abortion or sterilization.

The woman demanded to see our identification and her friends start-ed yelling at Namgyal. Tenzin explained that the woman wanted to return to her family and that she was afraid to talk with us; if any Chinese "spies" saw us together, she and her family would be in danger. I sensed that she wanted to talk with us, but that her friends clearly did not.

"Perhaps tomorrow," Namgyal said.

Tenzin started walking back to the monastery. He complained that the reception officers were not working hard enough and said that he wanted to see if his friends from school had arrived. I said that we would get our best interviews on our own and likened the process to a hunt. Tenzin liked this metaphor. He said hello to the monks we passed and stopped to help a man draw a bucket of water from a well. At the end of a row of army tents we passed a couple boiling tea. The woman was obviously pregnant. Within minutes we were drinking tea and hearing at length about the Nepalese police who had extracted bribes at eight different checkpoints.

"Yangzum was five months' pregnant when she went to the hospital for a check-up," Tenzin translated. "The Chinese doctor told her to have an injection to kill her baby. Yangzum refused. 'The hospital does not have the authority to force me to have an abortion,' she told them. She went home and escaped before the police could bring her back to the hospital."

*   *   *

Tenzin's mother found a Tibetan woman, Dolma, who was an obstetrician from Amdo and had undergone an abortion herself. Because Dr. Dolma had been educated in Chinese and worked in a Chinese hospital, she spoke Chinese better than Tibetan. Tenzin conducted her interview in Chinese. When Dr. Dolma became pregnant for the second time the head of her hospital told her to have an abortion or lose her job. She had the abortion.

She described her abortion in medical detail: the dilation of her cervix; the insertion of the curette; the scraping of her uterus; the fetal parts clogging the suction tube. The doctor who performed her abortion was Chinese. No medicines were prescribed for her because she did not experience any complications other than back pain for one month. She returned to work the next day.

Tenzin was in tears. He had never heard of these things before, and his weeping clearly embarrassed him. At this moment I realized how much my medical training had changed me. Just like Dr. Dolma herself, I was distant from her pain. I had to be in order to treat critically injured and sick people.

Besides the D&C abortion, which was virtually identical to the technique used in the West, Dr. Dolma said that women from four to nine months' pregnant were sometimes given an injection directly into their abdomen to induce abortion. During the five years that she had worked at the Chinese hospital, she said that she had seen 1,600 abortions by D&C, 400 by injection, and 800 sterilizations.

Tenzin laughed unexpectedly as he translated Dr. Dolma's account of how the doctor performing a sterilization makes a small cut in a woman's stomach. Dr. Dolma gave him a stern look. "They make a bigger cut if the woman is fat," he said. It took longer for Tenzin to learn the medical terms for sterilization than it took Dr. Dolma to perform such an operation: fifteen minutes. When I asked how the operation could be done so quickly, Dr. Dolma replied that everything was done under local anesthetic. This was painful, but the woman could walk home afterward.

* * *

Tenzin chopped vegetables for our dinner on the dirty cement floor while *ama-la*, as he called his mother, sat on the bed. Her feet were tired from going to each camp to make sure the Indian officials brought people water. *Ama-la* and grandmother-la let *amchi-la* (doctor), as they called me, sit on the bed and write my notes. "Varanasi was closed today," *ama-la* said. "There were two murders in the student quarter last night. I tried to go to the Ganges this morning but it was impossible. There is a curfew after the sun goes down."

The grandmother watched me writing in my journal. Even though she could not read English I still felt self-conscious. A cockroach scurried across the floor. Without thinking I raised my foot to crush the insect. The grandmother shrieked and jumped up and grabbed my leg before it could come down on this defenseless creature. Tenzin and his mother broke into hysterics as the grandmother berated me.

That night, lying on a bed of straw, I wrapped a sheet around my head to tune out the mosquitoes' buzzing. A truckload of Ladakhis who arrived in the middle of night kept everyone at the Sarnath Monastery up with their yelling and screaming. Between the Ladakhis and the mosquitoes I was kept awake worrying that I would not get enough interviews. This fear proved to be unfounded.

* * *

As the time approached for the Dalai Lama to deliver the Kalachakra, Tenzin lost his fear of talking to officials and asking women intimate questions about their reproductive anatomy. Busloads of jubilant refugees arrived every night. Although the majority of new arrivals were monks, and most left the camp after breakfast to see the sights in Sarnath, we easily obtained eight first-hand accounts from women who had experienced abortions and sterilizations. One woman who worked in a Chinese bookshop had been given two abortions because she had not waited three years after her first baby. Two women were sterilized after they delivered a healthy baby, only to see a nurse kill it with an injection in the soft spot on the forehead.

Some of the reasons women gave us as to why they were sterilized included not wanting to pay a fine; coming from a poor family; having to obey the Chinese rules; and having husbands who worked in Chinese cadres and were not allowed to have more than one child. Regardless of the reasons, the emotional toll this policy wreaked was reflected in increased numbers of divorces and families separating.

From my perspective, it was apparent that all of these women attributed their abortions and sterilizations to social, economic, and political sanctions against unauthorized children that were coercive in nature and existed on a pressure continuum. Regional variation accounted for differences in the amounts of fines, the numbers of children urban and rural families were allowed, and the length of time women who worked in a cadre had to wait between their first and second children. However, the individual accounts were similar in their details, and these accounts were drawn from women who came from throughout Tibet.

Many of the interviewees said their local Chinese officials were corrupt, and gave examples of Chinese women who paid bribes to get ration cards for extra children. Tibetans could also bribe officials, but most of them thought this was easier for the Chinese immigrants.

As with any investigation, questions led to more questions. All of the six Tibetans I interviewed who were from Amdo (northeastern Tibet) knew of or had seen mobile birth-control teams; the question now was whether these teams operated outside of Amdo. While all of the refugees said that Chinese hospitals had a dual system of health care, this was difficult to prove. Without an on-site investigation, it was impossible to discern how extensively China was implementing enforced family planning in rural Tibet.

* * *

A train with people sitting on its roof ran over an Indian beggar as it passed the new arrivals camp one morning. Tenzin and I saw the one-legged beggar hobbling toward the tracks on homemade crutches. He did not seem to be paying any attention to the oncoming train—but I never would have thought he would attempt to cross the tracks. The conductor did not slow down or blow the horn. The man did not make a sound as he flew through the air, landing with his arms and leg crumpled in unnatural positions.

Hundreds of people ran to him simultaneously, including a Tibetan doctor from the clinic. Massive lacerations covered the man's head. Part of his upper lip and nose were gone. Both arms were twisted backward like chicken wings. The remaining leg was severed below the knee, except for a shred of muscle that held the calf to the thigh. I put a tourniquet on the leg, which would have to be amputated. The Tibetan doctor wrapped gauze around the deeper lacerations. Tenzin recruited a rickshaw and five Indian men climbed aboard with the mortally wounded man and drove off. The man would probably die on the way to the hospital. I felt guilty for not going with him, but I had urgent work at the new arrivals camp.

We had our busiest day ever. In addition to a first-hand account of a mobile birth-control team, which took women by force for abortions and sterilization, we interviewed one woman who had been sterilized after her second child, and another who had an abortion because she had not applied for permission to have a child. Two nuns from Chudson nunnery in Lhasa recounted in horrid detail how dogs bit them at Gutsa Prison in April of 1988. Tenzin and I took turns staring blankly out of the tent over the parched fields.

Then, as we were about to leave, one of the nuns told us that she had been gang-raped. Immediately after her release from Gutsa she had returned to her nunnery, but they refused to take her back. Five Chinese men were waiting for her when she left the nunnery at dusk. Two of the men held her down while the rest took turns raping her. They put her clothes over her eyes so she could not see them. She was afraid to tell the police because she feared they might send her back to prison.

● ● ●

The Dalai Lama's arrival was postponed from 11:30 in the morning of December 20 until late that afternoon. By noon 100,000 people lined the streets from Sarnath to Varanasi. The Indian police beat the crowd back with bamboo *lakhis* to clear a passageway for the Dalai Lama's entourage. People fought to glimpse His Holiness waving from inside his car. The Dalai Lama's arrival meant the end of my work. All of the Tibetans would be at the Kalachakra during the day. At night everyone would want to eat and tend to their own needs.

Some day, I thought, I too would hear the teachings on the path toward compassion, but first I had to finish my report on sterilization. I longed to return home to my family for the Christmas holidays. Dust hung in the air like fog, a product of the overcrowding and lack of rain. Every day more Tibetans needed more water, food, shelter, and latrines. The tiny hamlet of Sarnath had turned into a disaster area. Soon contaminated water would begin causing widespread hepatitis and dysentery.

The man at the Potala Tours travel agency booth in Sarnath said that all of the train seats to Delhi had been booked for weeks. With Tenzin's help, I learned that indeed all of the seats had been booked, but also discovered that a fifty-rupee service charge could get me a second-class sleeper on the Super Deluxe train to Delhi that left at 8:00 that night. It would be a race to get back to the monastery for my things and then return to the Varanasi station for my train.

In the midst of my goodbyes to Tenzin's family, a heavy-set Tibetan man carrying bags of apples and bananas walked into the room. At first I did not recognize him, but it turned out to be Tsering, the Nepalese man I had treated in Lhasa who had been shot through the leg. He was thirty pounds heavier than when I had last seen him—we both were. I had not been able to do anything about the bullet that had torn through his leg, but my antibiotics had saved his life. His uncle had recognized me in the recent arrivals camp. His mother insisted that he bring us the fruit.

"You look younger," Tsering said, and I repeated the same to him. He said that he had no residual problems with his leg and jogged regularly. He also told me I had a place to stay in Kathmandu any time. Tsering recounted how he had spent three more months in Lhasa. "My sister filed a lawsuit against China for shooting me," Tenzin said. "The court confiscated my passport. It took months for them to find that I had been hit by a stray bullet. I had to write an extensive self-criticism before they let me go."

Just as I was leaving for the train station, Tica Broch was arriving from Switzerland. I recognized her from the hearing at the German Parliament where I had testified. Tica lobbied for Tibet at the United Nations and became excited about the prospect of my report on coerced abortion and sterilization.

"Everyone in Geneva has copies of John Ackerly's report on the suppression of religion," Tica said. "China threatened to pull out of the anti-Iraq coalition because of it. Just wait until they get wind of this sterilization report. If you can get it to me by February, it could make an international scene at the United Nations High Commission on Human Rights. Your article in the *Washington Post* on the mobile birth-control teams in Amdo infuriated China. The United Nations refused China's report on human rights in Tibet because of it."

Tenzin gave me the gift of a *khata* as we ran first to the wrong end of the train, then all the way back to the front car as the train started moving. People fought to get on and push their luggage through the windows. The aisle was so crowded that it took me ten minutes to maneuver to my sleeping berth, where a family from Calcutta was already ensconced. Despite the derogatory remarks directed at me from everyone in the compartment, I was invigorated to know that a man I had treated three years ago had lived, and that my article on human rights violations in Tibet had put pressure on China. Individual travelers can make a difference.

CHAPTER THIRTEEN

RETURN TO TIBET

JOHN SPENT FIVE weeks in Tibet in the summer of 1991 interviewing Chinese officials and Tibetans in eastern Kham (western Yunnan and Sichuan provinces) and Amdo (western Gansu and Qinghai provinces). Three weeks later he submitted a report on religious freedom, education, and population transfer to the United Nations High Commission on Human Rights. I had finished my report on China's family-planning policy in Tibet, entitled "Tibetans Under The Knife," but the refugees' accounts of coerced abortions and sterilizations that it contained lacked the veracity of John's on-site investigations. It was as though John and I were climbing. He had completed a new lead; I had to follow. John loaned me his hand-held video camcorder to use on my second trip to Tibet, this time in the winter of 1991.

I funded the trip with my savings from eight months of full-time work as a general practitioner, and hired another physician to staff the clinic during my absence. I planned to first travel overland for two months in Kham and Amdo before heading to Lhasa. Irony permeated my planning of the trip. I knew that all of the money I spent in Tibet would essentially subsidize the Chinese occupation. Also, four decades of Chinese colonization in Kham and Amdo, and the profusion of different Tibetan dialects, made it more practical for me to have a translator who spoke Chinese rather than Tibetan.

A friend at the International Lawyers Committee for Tibet recommended that I hire Jan, an American woman who had lived in China for seven years, written her graduate thesis at Berkeley on China's "minorities," and currently worked as a Chinese translator in San Francisco.

179

During a brief phone conversation I told Jan about my previous experience in Tibet, and promised her that we would not get arrested. She agreed to join me.

In Hong Kong, an extra $10 paid to a discount Kowloon travel agent expedited our receiving a three-month Chinese visa the next day. The hundreds of soldiers directing travelers around Chengdu Airport in western China set the tone for our first contact with the mainland. Most were young and unarmed and laughed often among themselves. One woman soldier stopped giggling long enough to check our visas, and then we were whisked to a cab. This gave me a false sense of confidence, until the manager at the luxury hotel we had selected saw the two of us coming through the marble lobby with our backpacks. I asked in English for a room. Predictably, none were available. Jan asked again, this time in the most polite form of Mandarin, and we miraculously had a suite on an empty wing, where two hall-monitor types kept up a twenty-four-hour watch.

At the hotel bar, Chinese men in gray suits whispered into obvious wires on the lapels of their coats as they surveyed the prostitutes, American military contractors, and businessmen who filled the room. We had a drink with a French travel agent named Pierre. Within minutes of introducing himself, and after learning that Jan and I were "cousins," and not a couple, he was offering to fly us illegally into Tibet.

"I am going to fly five Italians to Garze Monastery by helicopter," Pierre said. "It is a fantastic place. I would like to stay there for months. The Italians are arriving from Hong Kong tomorrow. I have arranged a deal with a general to let us rent a military helicopter that has just arrived from the United States. When the general heard that they were paying $5,000 each, he agreed to take a cut. This is our test flight. You are welcome to come with us for free," he added, smiling lasciviously at Jan.

I would have gone on the helicopter, but Pierre's assurances turned out to be less than reliable. The hotel's three travel agents all said they could arrange a jeep to drive us through Kham, but this was "*tai gui*" (too expensive), and every town I wanted to visit was a "minority area," which meant that it was closed to travelers.

It took me another day to learn that the hotel's Golden Dragon travel company was really run for profit by the military. In a back room I inadvertently glimpsed a man putting a two-inch stack of hundred-dollar bills into a wooden drawer. He wore a gray business suit. Seeing us, he introduced himself as the general in charge. He did not seem to realize that I had seen the money. Jan asked in Chinese if he had been stationed in Chengdu long. She listened with interest when he said that he had been the first Chinese man to cross the Karakoram Highway. We also learned from him that Golden Dragon could issue us any permit we wanted—for a price.

The general led us to an adjacent room and introduced us to the manager, who insisted that we use her English name of Lois. "Several months ago," Lois said, "an American couple caused trouble for us." Lois described at length how the Americans had brought "shame" on Golden Dragon for interviewing Tibetans and writing "untrue" things in the press. I presumed that the Americans she was referring to must have been John and his translator. I promised to not cause trouble and started bargaining. Lois wanted $200 for every day we rented a new Toyota jeep, which came with an obligatory driver and guide. " *Tai gui*," Jan said.

After an hour of negotiation, I signed a contract agreeing to pay $1,080 for ten days in a military jeep. Lois called at seven the next morning. She had gotten our travel permits, but informed me that I would have to pay an extra 100 FEC (thirty U.S. dollars) for three non-driving days that we would have the jeep. Jan and I immediately headed to the Golden Dragon office, where we started arguing with Lois. "I did not calculate exactly," Lois said. "There is no profit in it for me."

"That's your problem," I said, and then reminded her of our contract.

"I have not actually gotten your permits," Lois said.

Jan tried to intervene, but then I unleashed the ultimate insult: "By being dishonest, you are losing face," I shot at Lois.

Lois screamed at me in Chinese. I did not need a translation to know that she had canceled our trip. I explained to her contritely that I didn't care about the extra money, but the principle. I took a perverse pleasure in repeatedly taking Lois to the limit, apologizing, and then resuming my attack. Later that afternoon we finally signed another contract.

* * *

Our Chinese driver, Mr. Chu, had an untamed mop of thick, dark hair that seemed permanently windblown. He had learned Tibetan as a child when he had accompanied his father, who was also a driver, on trips all over Tibet. He told us that he had many Tibetan friends, and that Americans gave the best tips. Neither Mr. Chu nor our guide, Zhou, minded Jan's request that they not smoke in the vehicle. I felt an immediate affection for both of them, despite the obstacles they might represent for my work.

Zhou was twenty-two years old and had never been to any of the towns where we would be traveling. He also spoke fluent English, which made me suspect that he was a policeman. A few minutes into the trip we struck a bond when he said that his mother, father, and older sister were all obstetricians. He had decided to become a guide, he told us, because doctors had to work too much.

I was surprised to see so many construction projects on the fertile plains, with thousands of people shoveling sand and gravel along the river as we wound into the barren mountains. I counted the trucks that came barreling down the steep, winding road carrying what appeared to be old-growth logs. There were 200 of them before I stopped counting. When Jan asked where all the logs were coming from, Zhou said, "From the West."

"You mean Tibet," I said.

"Tibet is part of China," Zhou corrected.

We drove through hundreds of kilometers of Kham's denuded valleys. Dust choked the air, a product of fallow fields stripped of their root systems. Scarce stands of mature pine were the only reminder of the region's once-great forests. The lone trees on the ridges stood out like fossilized dinosaur spines. Again I started counting trucks carrying timber to the mainland, and again I lost track after reaching 200.

● ● ●

After a few days Jan got bronchitis from the dust. The prospect of Jan being ill made me realize how dependent I was on her language skills to find and interview Tibetans, as well as to negotiate for food and places to stay. Unfortunately, none of the local Police Security Bureau (PSB) officials knew we were coming, as Lois had promised, so we had to deal with prolonged bouts of intrusive questioning. Because we were traveling in "closed" towns, Jan had to put up with a lot of "*mei you*" (don't have) before finding any hotels that would take foreigners. Invariably, our rooms looked out over construction sites where stone-crushing equipment clanked until 4:00 A.M. When the cacophony finally stopped, the roosters would start crowing. This pattern primed us for our first fight with Zhou.

"I have to be with you at all times," Zhou said when we first tried to take a walk alone through a Tibetan town. "You are not allowed to leave the hotel without me. You are not allowed to talk to Tibetans about anything political."

Jan, nervous and worn out from her illness, burst into tears upon hearing Zhou's reprimand and walked away. Zhou did not know how to respond. At a loss, he yelled for her to come back, but she kept going. I felt sorry for him. Jan had given his male ego a good beating. "Now you've done it," I said sardonically, slapping Zhou on the back. I left in the opposite direction. Zhou retreated to his room to sulk.

I hurried into town and met up with Jan in the market, where we agreed to take advantage of the opportunity and go to the local People's Hospital. "If Zhou finds out," Jan said, "I'll tell him you needed medicine for the *douza* (diarrhea)."

We made it to the hospital at noon and waited for an hour in an anteroom while the doctors had their lunch. A pale, elderly Tibetan man patted the bench next to him and we sat down. Dirt caulked the cracks in his trousers and calloused hands. He was obviously a farmer and communicated with us through his twenty-four-year-old daughter, who spoke Chinese. I learned that he came from a nearby village, and he said that he had been suffering from a cough and pain in his right chest for a month, which was why he was here at the hospital. He also told us that he had seven children between the ages of eighteen and forty-two years old.

Jan asked how it was that he could have had so many children. He explained that the Chinese didn't start family planning in Tibet until 1989. Now there was a 2,000-yuan fine for extra children. Our brief conversation confirmed what I had learned from interviewing refugees: there was regional variation in many aspects of China's family-planning policy in Tibet. Jan was reluctant to ask the father and daughter about abortions, but she did. Both of us were surprised when the daughter said casually that all Chinese hospitals did abortions and sterilizations, and that most of the women in her village had been sterilized.

Within minutes of entering the People's Hospital I came upon a room with four Chinese women internists huddled around a pot-belly stove. Jan introduced me as a *meiguo daifu* (Western doctor). I said that in the United States internists were the most intelligent doctors. Jan translated this and the women smiled; apparently, this was also true in China.

The two-child policy for minority women had been changed this year, the internists told us after they stopped giggling. Now minority women who lived in towns could have only one child, just like Chinese women. I asked them about contraceptives and the doctors said that Tibetans didn't like interfering with conception. Abortion for any reason was anathema to their religious beliefs.

"For these reasons," Jan translated, "many Tibetan women would rather be sterilized than have an abortion or use contraception." The implications of their statement saddened me; the coercive nature of this policy had even more profound implications for the Tibetans than I had assumed.

* * *

The day after our confrontation, Zhou could not look Jan in the eyes. During the night Jan and I had worked out a strategy to become super tourists. Our plan was to wear Zhou down with sightseeing at the next few towns so he would want to leave us alone, enabling us to conduct our interviews. We dove into our roles with enthusiasm.

Several nights later, while resting at a truck stop, Mr. Chu, Zhou, Jan, and I drank rum and warmed our hands over the electric wire heater we used for boiling tea. Zhou's face reddened after one sip of rum. He soon asked me to arm wrestle. I pretended at first not to be interested, then beat him handily. He pouted until I challenged him to do pull-ups on the door jamb. Zhou did three. I stopped at fifteen.

A local PSB officer barged into the room. I offered him a mug of dark rum. He sucked the black liquid enthusiastically through his decaying teeth and told us that he was fifty years old. Twenty years ago, when the army first sent him to this outpost, Tibetans wore animal skins without undergarments. I thought we were in for a lecture on the backward Tibetans, but the official said that he took pride in the local customs and had learned the local dialect. He encouraged us to return in late July and early August for a festival at which thousands of nomads congregated for horse races, dancing, and drinking.

After gulping his second rum he expressed his exasperation that a foreigner who had traveled here the previous year had written an article about how backward the area was. This had hurt him because he had seen how the local economy had improved. The official stood up and left as suddenly as he had entered. Although he did not return, his intrusion fed my growing fear that we would never have enough privacy in Tibet to do our research.

Mr. Chu said that some Tibetans had picked up bad Chinese habits, like cheating other people. He attributed this to Tibet having been taken over by China. Tibetans, he said, were compassionate, kind people. They seemed backward to those Chinese who didn't have religion. The Chinese who had experienced contact with the Tibetans were richer spiritually.

Hearing both this Chinese official and Mr. Chu tell us that they genuinely liked the Tibetans enlivened me. The Chinese were learning compassion from the Tibetans. Zhou smiled broadly and offered us the use of the jeep, "for free," for an extra day's drive to Lanzhou. "I will personally show you the sights," he told us.

Mr. Chu agreed and we all drank. I said that when I was Zhou's age I had realized that my own government could not always be trusted. I mentioned Watergate as an example.

"Irangate," Zhou added confidently. "About Tiananmen Square, I don't know what the truth is."

"A lot of demonstrators were killed," I said.

"We can discuss these things among ourselves," Zhou said. "Not with foreigners."

* * *

Hundreds of thousands of yaks and sheep grazed on the plains as we crossed into Amdo a few days later. We spent an entire day driving on a dirt track and stopped often for yaks to get out of the way. Noble-looking men and women with one child on the back of their horses tended expansive flocks. Zhou was in a good mood and shared a large bag of cookies with the Tibetan families we passed riding yaks and walking barefoot through the fresh snow.

We were snowed in for three days in a small town. The fashionable Tibetans there wore leopard collars around their sheepskin coats. Zhou reluctantly agreed to accompany us to the local Tibetan hospital, where we found a Tibetan physician in his office on the second floor. He wore long underwear and a sweater beneath his soiled white coat.

Jan asked questions in Chinese. The Tibetan doctor's name was Tenzin. He represented the seventh generation of physicians in his family, a heritage that had been passed from father to son. Before 1980, when the Chinese built the hospital, sick Tibetans had come to the doctor's home. Now every township in Amdo had a Chinese-built hospital. Tenzin dreamed that in ten to fifteen years the Tibetans would have a major teaching hospital where local doctors could hone their skills. Although there was a Tibetan medical school 30 miles away in Aba with thirty students, most of the Tibetan physicians still learned medicine from their fathers.

By the time we finally got around to discussing family planning, Zhou was completely bored. In rural villages Tibetans were allowed to have three children, one more than the women from the local Hui and Chiang minority communities. As in Kham, many Tibetan women chose to be sterilized rather than face a fine of 2,000 yuan.

Tenzin surprised me by saying that many Tibetans had developed a greater sense of reproductive responsibility. They understood that with the privilege of being able to create life came a responsibility not to have more children than the environment could support. I asked him if Tibetan medicine had any birth-control pills and Tenzin replied that they did, but they were not 100-percent effective. Most Tibetan physicians advised their patients to abstain from intercourse from the twelfth day of a woman's cycle to the end of her next period.

After we left I asked Zhou if he had a preference for a male child. He laughed. "When I was in university," he said. "I joked with my friends that having a girl was bad. But I did not really feel that way. In cities everyone wants their child to prosper. This means having only one.

Otherwise there will not be enough resources to go around. In urban areas people understand this. In villages they have backward beliefs. This is a matter of education."

Later that same day Jan and I snuck back to the hospital on our own. This time we met two Chinese women obstetricians in a room identified as the "Family Planning Office." Jan introduced me to them as an American obstetrician and the three of us compared the contraceptive techniques used in our respective countries. The doctors said they had prescribed both IUDs and birth-control pills. They also sometimes used hormonal implants that prevented ovulation for from three to six months, but these also caused side effects like giddiness and blood clots. They also told us that most Tibetan women chose to be sterilized in order to comply with the family-planning policy.

The women doctors sat up proudly when Jan translated my statement that Chinese women had more options for family planning than Western women. In China, the doctors explained, they could do D&C's up to four months after conception, and injections of levanor, which induces abortion, up to eight months. They claimed that they routinely performed tubal ligations that took no longer than fifteen minutes.

"What happens if the infant comes out alive?" I asked.

"They are given an injection of alcohol into the anterior fontanel [the soft spot on a newborn's forehead] or submerged in water," Jan said. "In China, this is considered abortion."

* * *

We spent our last evening roasting yak meat on the heater and drinking *baiju* (rice wine). I turned the television on at ten, when the news was broadcast in English, and was surprised to hear the commentator denouncing George Bush. "The People's Republic of China condemns George Bush for interfering in China's internal affairs," she said. "Today the U.S. president signed the State Department Appropriations Bill that recognizes Tibet as an occupied country."

Mr. Chu and Zhou were excited about finally returning from the countryside to their homes. Mr. Chu stopped often to purchase freshly killed rabbit, three pheasant, and quail. Zhou refused to take a 200-

yuan tip I pressed on him when we got back to our hotel in Lanzhou. "We are friends," he insisted, holding my hand in his fist. We embraced, and I forced the money into his pocket. Mr. Chu gladly took the money I offered him and volunteered to drive for us again anytime. Jan organized the farewell photo. She messed Zhou's and my hair. There was no need to mess Mr. Chu's hair.

* * *

We soon learned that no permits were needed to travel in Gansu province. I was glad to hear this, because China had instituted its eugenics program in Gansu, where mentally handicapped women were sterilized to improve the "quality of the race." Here I began using John's video camera. I had an aversion to pointing a camera in anyone's face, and I knew I would be in situations where I wanted to film people discreetly. I worked on shooting the camera from the hip, obscuring it under a loose shirt or jacket. I practiced on slogans painted in six-foot characters on the town's adobe walls: ABORTION IS NOT OUTSIDE OF FAMILY PLANNING; AN OVERGROWN POPULATION CAN BE OPPRESSIVE; FAMILY PLANNING IS EVERYONE'S RESPONSIBILITY.

Jan was sick again when we arrived at our hotel and needed to rest. This left me at a real disadvantage, but I tried to buoy my spirits with the thought that every hospital we had visited so far had contained at least one physician who could speak English. I had also learned how to introduce myself in Chinese as an obstetrician, and how to ask essential questions.

I went to the local People's Hospital and met Dr. Chang, a friendly young pediatrician whose English improved the more we talked. I said in Chinese that I treated babies, and he showed off for me all of his patients: three infants, all less than a year old, all admitted for rehydration. The children were plugged into well-used intravenous lines. I shuddered later when I saw the nurses refill the glass bottles with boiled water; if the children survived their rehydration, they could very well die from disseminated yeast and bacterial infections spread by way of the IV lines.

For an hour Dr. Chang translated into English the captions to the pictures in the pediatrics textbook in his office. I had not realized at first that he was Tibetan, and that though he could speak Chinese, and even a little English, he could not speak his native tongue. Jan confirmed this the next day when she returned with me. Dr. Chang had been sent to Lanzhou at the age of five, where he had lived until he had graduated from medical school two years before. He was twenty-three.

He did not realize that the video camera I had placed an arm's length away from him on his desk was filming him as he explained China's two-child policy for Tibetans. I realized that filming anyone without their consent could be seen as unethical. I also felt strongly that China's coercive family-planning policy, like its oppressive occupation of Tibet, had to be exposed before it could be stopped. Dr. Chang blushed when I asked what happened to babies who were still alive after an abortion. I rephrased the question and he shook his head. He would not answer.

The next day, when a recovered Jan told him that I was an obstetrician, Dr. Chang took us to a conference room and recruited a tall friend of his who was also an obstetrician, as well as an internist who chain-smoked cigarettes, to talk with us. Each of the three were mesmerized when Jan spoke, enough so that none of them noticed the sound of the video camera's small lens turning automatically as it focused. I aimed at the obstetrician when he said, "In cities they can offer IUDs. In minority areas sterilization is the only form of birth control." When he bragged that he could do a tubal ligation in ten minutes, and had once done forty in one day, I could not resist looking down at the camera to make certain it was recording. I was mortified to see that it was not.

The chain-smoking internist explained in English that family planning was more lax in distant villages, where Tibetans were known to have three or more children, while in big cities like Lanzhou, women could have only one child. Most of the people in this area were minorities: Hui, Tu, Chiang, and Tibetans.

"What do you do with handicapped women?" I asked.

"Eugenics is part of China's national family-planning policy," the internist said. "The national government says that women who are diagnosed as being mentally ill are to be sterilized." When asked how he diagnosed mental illness he replied, "We ask questions in simple terms in order to determine their intelligence."

Before our meeting ended, I did not get to find out if a Tibetan woman who could not read or speak Chinese was at greater risk of sterilization. I also had not yet witnessed a procedure. Still, I should have known better than to return to the same hospital for a third time. Dr. Chang was not as pleased to see me, but he helped me look for an obstetrician. We found the head of the obstetrics department in the hall. He said that Dr. Chang's friend was away visiting small villages today. Dr. Chang asked if I could see a tubal ligation and the chief berated him. "This hospital does not do operations," Dr. Chang said sadly. "I'm afraid you are not allowed here. You must leave immediately."

* * *

We took his advice. Luckily, the bus driver stopped for anyone on the road who hailed him, regardless of how packed the bus had become. I was squashed next to a Tibetan woman and her cherubic daughter, who wore matching enormous corduroy overcoats. This left half of me hanging out into the aisle, battling hands and elbows. Jan had brought along a washboard to insulate her feet from the freezing metal floorboards; we had known setting out that since we would now be traveling by bus in rural Tibet, we would need to employ more sophisticated survival techniques.

The first pass offered vistas of distant curtains of rock. Herds of yaks, sheep, and wild horses grazed freely on the hills. We followed a red dirt track into a canyon. In one adobe settlement our Chinese driver had to slow down for a group of Tibetan women herding sheep through the road. He leaned on the horn and spat at the women as he plowed forward and scattered their sheep.

* * *

In the next town, we walked right into the obstetrics wing of the People's Hospital and met five female Tibetan obstetricians. I put the video on wide angle and asked why there were no male obstetricians here. Jan and the doctors laughed at me. "Cultural barriers prohibit a Chinese man from being with a minority woman," Jan translated.

A young obstetrician named Dr. Xian did most of the talking. Like most of the other Tibetan physicians we had met, these obstetricians could scarcely communicate with their Tibetan patients unless they spoke Chinese. After we compared different methods of abortion, Dr. Xian said that all obstetricians routinely performed abortions and sterilizations. I asked if I could observe an operation.

"*Mei wonti*" (no problem), she said, and told us to return at two that afternoon.

I was so excited that I had a difficult time paying attention to Dr. Xian saying that Amdo had special teams of doctors and nurses that only visited remote areas. These mobile birth-control teams traveled year-round to educate nomads and villagers about diet, contraception, and family planning. The mobile teams performed abortions and sterilizations according to a two-child policy. The procedures were free; women had to pay for medicine.

• • •

Dr. Xian washed and dried her hands with a soiled rag before leading us into a room where a woman lay naked on a table with her legs spread in stirrups. Dr. Xian wore a surgical mask and draped a filthy cloth over the woman's pelvis that exposed her vagina.

Shooting from the hip allowed me to capture the scene in graphic detail as Dr. Xian did a pelvic examination. The nurse handed instruments wrapped in a stained cloth to Dr. Xian. The patient moaned when Dr. Xian inserted the speculum and sounded the uterus with a metal wire. She pinched the cervix with forceps and pulled it up to insert the curette. I began to feel hot. I had gotten so accustomed to cold weather that I now habitually wore silk underwear beneath a union suit, a wool shirt, and the jacket I wore to conceal the camera. I tried to unbutton my shirt and long underwear as discreetly as possible. Sweat beaded on my forehead as Dr. Xian scraped the inside of the uterus and the products of conception sucked through the clear plastic tubing.

When large droplets of sweat began cascading off my forehead and upper lip, I knew I was about to pass out. The woman's moaning made me think of all women in Tibet, and China, who were undergoing these mechanical, unsanitary, coerced abortions. With the blood draining from my head, I staggered white and shaking out of the operating room. I lay down on a bench outside. A Tibetan man there looked at me as though seeing overdressed Western men staggering out of operating rooms on the brink of losing consciousness was normal.

I was sitting upright again when Dr. Xian came out to see what had happened to me. Jan told her that the procedure they used was just the same in the United States, and that I left because I had wanted to respect the woman's privacy.

• • •

As we walked up the hill to town, I realized that I had gathered enough material for my report. I needed to get to Lhasa, and knew that this meant I could no longer keep my promise to not get arrested. Jan realized this too. She agreed to accompany me to Xining by bus, from which I would continue alone to Lhasa.

I stopped to talk with two Tibetan families waiting in a wagon behind a tractor. "*Tashi delek. Nga America amchi yin*" (Hello, I'm an American doctor), I said. Most of the Tibetans on the cart looked at me trying to figure out what I had just said. A woman with two children on her lap understood. "*Lhasa-kay*" (Lhasa dialect), she said, and explained to me that "hello" in the Amdo dialect was, "*Cho day moo, nee ya.*"

I told her that I was thirty-three years old. She said I looked older. When she said she was twenty-nine years old, I said she looked younger. Changing the subject deftly, I asked, "*Chop-chup, doogay?*" (Sterilization, you have?) The woman said yes, she had been sterilized after having her second child at the local People's Hospital.

Although I did not have the Chinese and Tibetan language skills necessary to conduct a thorough interview, this encounter showed me that I could still glean some information on my own. I could also still try to get footage of a sterilization being performed in an operating room. As it turned out, I needed this newfound optimism to enter the land of *mei you* on my own.

When we reached Xining, the travel agent at the hotel said that the road from Golmud to Lhasa was closed: nine Westerners had died when a bus overturned. I abandoned the notion of taking a bus or hitchhiking to Lhasa and instead returned to Chengdu by train with Jan.

• • •

Except for the speakers playing socialist tunes and propaganda at high volume, I loved sleeping on Chinese trains. Even our two compartment-mates, I noticed, seemed to dislike the intrusion. I waited for the two men to step out to smoke; fortunately, we did not have to wait long. Jan guarded the door while I liberated seven three-and-one-half-inch screws before each speaker fell forward and exposed the two essential wires. Clipping them, I felt a momentary surge of nostalgia-inducing adrenaline.

I found an Englishman on the train whom I had met in Dharamsala. He traveled under a Tibetan name, Nema, because he wanted to return to Tibet in the future. Nema shared Lanzhou *pijou* with us and told me the latest traveler stories.

"Two dozen foreigners are stranded in Golmud," Nema told us. "No one is getting through. One Dutchman shaved his head and disguised himself as a monk, but the police caught him and turned him back. The truck drivers are afraid to lose their licenses if they are caught with a foreigner. One Frenchman supposedly hitchhiked to Lhasa. It took two weeks. He was so pissed off when he arrived that he would not speak to anyone for days."

Nema had come to Amdo to improve his Chinese and Tibetan and to buy books. His trip had been a success; he had bought seventy pounds' worth of books, so many that he was having trouble sending them all home.

The barren fields beside the train tracks made me feel detached. Patches of ice reminded me that I had not seen anything green for weeks. Winter was an ugly time to travel in Kham and Amdo.

"When George Bush did his seven-month stint as U.S. ambassador to Beijing," Nema said, "the Chinese had a difficult time pronouncing Bush. They referred to him as Ambassador Bushi, which means 'no' in Mandarin."

* * *

Back in Chengdu, I met Peter, a Canadian probation officer, and Anna, a Yugoslavian tour leader, at a travelers' hotel. They were planning a four-day trip to Lhasa, the shortest possible tour, and asked if I wanted to join them. It sounded good to me, but I had hopes of staying longer.

They said they wanted to stay longer too, but were en route to India. After paying $600 each, which included round-trip airfare, we celebrated at a pub.

There we met a gregarious Tibetan man named Puntso who asked us to sit with him and his *Rinpoche* (revered monk). He explained that the *Rinpoche* was the head of a large monastery in India. This was their first trip to China. Puntso led us to a large man wearing thick gold rings and a pinstriped suit who presided over a group of six Tibetans. The men wore suits. The women wore elegant silk *chubas.*

The *Rinpoche* barely acknowledged our presence when Puntso introduced us by our countries, as "Mister Canada, Miss Yugoslavia, and Doctor America." He gulped a glass of warm Coca-Cola before the ice in it could melt and immediately called out to the waiter for another. When I asked where his monastery was in India he replied, "I hate Americans."

Puntso laughed nervously. "*Rinpoche* does not hate Americans," he said.

"I hate all Westerners," the *Rinpoche* said. "The West sold out Tibet." One of the women burst into tears and pulled her coat over her head.

"If communism can fall in Eastern Europe, it can fall in China," I said.

"Tibet is finished," the *Rinpoche* shouted as he gulped another Coca-Cola. I looked at the angry, overweight man downing Coke and saw a diabetic on the verge of physical, emotional, and spiritual breakdown. I said resignedly that I hoped he was wrong and excused myself before losing my patience. If this had not been the eve of my return to Lhasa, I would have wanted to talk more with the despondent *Rinpoche.*

* * *

Once aloft, Peter and Anna each shot a roll of film before we landed in Lhasa. I too was moved by the snowcapped leviathans rising above the clouds, but I knew the mountains would look diminutive in their photos. Instead I pondered what Lhasa might hold for me this time. I wanted to find out what had happened to my patients in the Jokhang

Monastery, especially Champa Tenzin. I was also determined to video-tape a sterilization.

Landing in Gonggar Airport and having to walk through a gauntlet of soldiers with machine guns reinforced my plan to avoid our tour as much as possible. Andy, the English name of our pre-assigned guide, had no trouble picking out the only three foreigners on the flight. He was tall and friendly and fluent in English. He welcomed us to our black luxury sedan with dark tinted windows, the same car government officials used. "For the next three days the driver and I will take you wherever you want," he assured us. During the two-hour drive to Lhasa we learned that going "wherever you want" meant choosing between tours of the Potala Palace, the Ganden, Sera, and Jokhang monasteries, and a carpet factory. We were forbidden to go anywhere without Andy.

"In Yugoslavia we have more freedom than this," Anna said, demanding that Andy stop the car. "I want to take a photograph of that Tibetan village. Is that all right?"

"Whatever you wish," he said, feigning a smile.

"How long have you been in Lhasa?" I asked.

"Too long," Andy said. "First the government told me two years. Five years later I'm still here."

We stopped to take pictures of eleven Tibetans riding on a tractor cart, barley fields, and a gigantic image of the Buddha painted on a boulder. Instead of taking a picture of the Buddha, I photographed a military convoy in desert camouflage coming out of Lhasa: trucks packed with soldiers, more trucks towing artillery and anti-aircraft guns, chauffeured jeeps carrying officers in dark glasses. After the convoy passed I asked Andy what he thought of the Eastern European countries becoming independent.

"Russian communism was a proletarian revolution," Andy said. "The workers revolted because they wanted a higher standard of living. Chinese communism is a peasant revolution. In China, peasants have a good standard of living. Housing is free. So is health care and education. China will not revolt."

"What about Tibet?" I asked.

"Have you been to Tibet before?" Andy asked. I said that I had, but lied in telling him that I had last been here in 1986. He bought it.

"Maybe Tibetans will get independence," he said indifferently. "The longer I am in Tibet the more I want to go home."

We stopped at a military checkpoint outside the city limit. Andy relinquished our passports and permits to soldiers wearing riot helmets and AK-47s. Peter trembled when I aimed my camera from my lap and photographed a soldier peering inside our car. When we drove through Andy pointed out dozens of three- and four-story buildings under construction for Chinese settlers, including a war college campus of forty-three buildings, as though this would impress us.

Peter and Anna started arguing with Andy when we stopped at a sterile cement hotel. "This has nothing to do with Tibet," Anna complained, "and it costs ninety FEC, the same as the Holiday Inn." Andy said that it was too late to change. We should rest for two hours before going to Sera Monastery. I agreed.

When Andy left, I suggested to Peter and Anna that we head over to the Barkhor in the heart of Lhasa. They enthusiastically agreed, but began to look worried as we walked through mile after mile of housing complexes for Chinese immigrants. There were so many more buildings and Chinese in Lhasa since I'd last been here that I lost my bearings.

Finally, we stumbled into the Barkhor Square and its living stream of pilgrims circumambulating the Jokhang Temple. Peter and Anna were enchanted. They stopped so often to take pictures that I made plans to split off and meet them back at the hotel.

A quick stop at the Snowlands, Yak, Kiri, and Banak Shol hotels revealed that a dozen overland travelers were presently legally registered at the Yak Hotel, for only ten FEC a night. I took this information to the police station where I had previously gotten an "Alien Travel Permit." A plainclothes Tibetan man said he was in charge and demanded to know what I was doing in Lhasa. I said that "Golden Dragon" had arranged everything, and he relaxed immediately. I asked him if Lhasa was an open city. At first he said that all foreign guests had to be on a prearranged tour, but after further questioning he admitted, "Technically, Lhasa is an open city. All travel outside the city limits must be arranged in a tour." I thanked him and returned to my cement box of a hotel.

When Andy returned I told him that I needed to rest. He said that I would feel better tomorrow and whisked Peter and Anna away in the sedan.

* * *

I waited about ten minutes before heading out, taking a circuitous route to one of Lhasa's Chinese hospitals. I started walking along the river until I was sure that no one was following me, then cut through alleys to the main road. A bicycle rickshaw took me to the emergency room, where an intern directed me to the run-down women's building. I entered with the video camera filming from my hip.

A nurse shrieked and ran when she saw me. I followed her and soon came upon a Dr. Tashi, the oldest of the staff's four female Tibetan obstetricians. I stuck out my hand and introduced myself in Chinese. Using a combination of Chinese, Tibetan, English, and sign language, Dr. Tashi gave me a tour.

We started with the operating room, where three doctors were trying to start an intravenous line in a pale Tibetan woman's foot. Dr. Tashi said "hemoglobin" and scribbled a note to herself, "4%," on her hand. She explained that the woman was having a miscarriage and would have to have an abortion the next day.

Dr. Tashi led me into the next room, where she stopped at each bed to give a brief diagnosis that summarized the patient's condition. She introduced me to patients and their family members as an American obstetrician. Of the seven women in the room, I understood that two were there for *chop-chup* and one for *guaco* (abortion).

Some family members of hospital patients were cooking on the hospital's rooftop, where we could see the Potala Palace rising above the sprawling concrete suburbs. Dr. Tashi's tour ended in the doctors' lounge. We flirted mildly, comparing our ages and then discussing techniques for abortion and sterilization. She laughed when I said that I was single. I laughed when she said that she was married. She herself had one child and used an IUD, she said, but most Tibetan women had *chop-chup.*

* * *

The next morning, I told Andy that I was too sick to see Drepung Monastery. "I hope you feel better this afternoon," Andy said. "You will like the Potala Palace."

When I got to the Jokhang, the Barkhor was packed with nomads and villagers who had arrived in Lhasa on religious pilgrimages. I also noticed a few Chinese beggars from the mainland. I entered the monastery with a group of Italian tourists who made videotapes of Tibetans prostrating, monks chanting in the central courtyard, and pilgrims offering dollops of yak butter to butter lamps.

I waited to find a familiar face, then finally began wandering down a hall. I eventually came upon Sonam, whom Heidi and I had treated for burns in 1987. He hugged me and pointed to the absence of scars on his face. "*Yakbudoo*," he said, and left to find a translator. He returned with an English-speaking monk named Tenzin, whom I also remembered, and then began talking with manic intensity. Tenzin translated quickly to keep up with Sonam.

"In 1987," Tenzin translated, "the Jokhang had eighty monks. Twenty have since died, some in prison. Some ran away to India. Others are still in prison. Many people worry: in the future, maybe few monks. Maybe someday lost."

"We are workers in a museum," he continued. "We have no true religious freedom. If we had true religious freedom, then monasteries would be like schools. There would be students here, and knowledge persons. Today, people are only allowed to pray and offer butter. After that, nothing. In Buddhism, the most important thing is to learn. The scriptures are very deep. The first time you can't understand. After teaching and meditation you begin to understand. Today people only know how to practice."

A knock made Sonam go to the door, where he received a whispered message. Tenzin laughed when I hid my camera. "Champa Tenzin is waiting to see you," he said. Word of my arrival must have spread through the monastery. Tenzin also said that we had to be careful that spies did not see us. As they had so many times after the riot, monks led me across the many-tiered rooftops to a secluded room.

Grotesque scars covered Champa Tenzin's face, arms, and neck, but his eyes radiated a gentle strength. Before we started talking, he held up a picture of President Bush meeting the Dalai Lama, his smile breaking into an earsplitting grin. Through Tenzin, I learned that Champa's friends had taken him to the *Mendzekhang* several days after the October 1 riot. There the police interrogated him every day. After one month they took him to Sangyip Prison, where he was tortured; his burns proved to them that he was a "splittist agent of the Dalai Clique." The police beat him with cattle prods and put him on starvation rations, but he did not break. After one month they stopped beating him daily. When they let him out after four months he learned that the Panchen Lama had helped win his release.

Tenzin said that I had to leave before any spies noticed me. He told me to come back in two days and Champa Tenzin would have for me a tape recording of prisoners describing their treatment and what they thought of Chinese occupation.

"A Tibetan guard at Sangyip is making the tape now," Tenzin said. "It is important that it get out of Tibet safely."

I agreed and asked if Champa had anything he would like to say to people in other countries. "We need help from the world people," Tenzin translated. "We need freedom. We need independence from the Chinese."

* * *

Later, our sedan broke down halfway up the steep driveway to the back of the Potala. I forgot that I was supposed to be sick and walked ahead, faster than the tour. Peter and Anna listened attentively to Andy's tour-guide perversion of Tibetan history. I surreptitiously ducked under a canvas tarp and followed the sound of women singing down into a dusty courtyard, until my eyes gradually distinguished forms shoveling rubble amid the cloud of dust. This was the real Potala, still under reconstruction after all these years.

I rejoined Andy on the rooftop. He was ordering a Tibetan worker to find the key to the Dalai Lama's sleeping quarters. The worker replied in Chinese that he did not have the key. The man who did had gone for the day. "Tibetans are stupid," Andy said. I made a panorama with the video camera that showed the ocean of new concrete apartment buildings stretching toward the mountains up and down the valley; smokestacks pouring black soot into the air cast a haze in the air that rivaled that of Los Angeles.

I whispered in Tibetan to the worker that I was a doctor who had seen the Lhasa riots in 1987, and that the Chinese occupation was bad. His face brightened and he produced the key to the Dalai Lama's winter quarters from his pocket. When Andy came upon me photographing His Holiness's bed, with his robe folded just as he had left it in 1959, he said, "You must have good karma."

I said that I did, and took the opportunity to ask if I could extend my stay for two more days. Andy said this was impossible; he had already made our plane reservations. I mentioned the police captain who said I could stay at a Tibetan hotel as long as I did not leave the city limits. Andy refused again, but as he did so I noticed he was eyeing my 35-millimeter camera.

"This is a remarkable camera," I said.

"How much did you pay for it?" Andy asked.

I told him the truth: I had bought the camera in Hong Kong two months ago for $100, and I would sell it to him for seventy-five. We shook hands and went straight to the Golden Dragon office. Andy gave Peter and Anna their tickets and changed mine to leave two days later. Then he borrowed American dollars to pay me. All of this happened so quickly that I wished I had asked him for more money.

"Where are you staying?" Andy called as I left.

"A Tibetan hotel," I said.

"Call me if you need a guide."

• • •

A woman in the market recognized me, and as we talked she fought to hold back tears. Her husband had been in prison for two years along with another man I had known. The woman smiled when people greeted her on the street, but her face quickly resumed its sad expression.

"I can't trust anyone," she whispered. "More than a thousand plainclothes police are always on the streets." I wanted to reassure the woman that her husband would be all right, but this was not likely.

A Taiwanese woman doing laundry in the courtyard spoke enough English to communicate to me that she had hitchhiked here from

Chengdu. Every night the police caught her in town and sent her back east in the direction from which she had come. Every morning she got up early and hitchhiked west.

I met an Israeli couple who spoke English, but they were too preoccupied with getting out of Lhasa to help me. Their flight from Kathmandu to Chengdu had landed in Lhasa with engine trouble. The local PSB had questioned them for a few hours, then agreed to let them stay for a week. There were also several German hippies who had hitchhiked in from the Nepalese border. They knew Otto and told me he was due to arrive any week now. Otto still came to Lhasa every year. The passage of time allowed me to remember the wildman's spirit with fondness.

I went to sleep discouraged. However, the next afternoon I was recognized on the street by Rinchen, a Tibetan woman who had heard me address a demonstration at the United Nations in New York City. She asked me what I was doing in Lhasa. Within minutes she had agreed to go with me to the People's Hospital.

* * *

Rinchen gasped as we walked straight into the operating room at the People's Hospital. There we discovered Dr. Tashi putting a bandage over a vertical incision on a woman patient's pubic region. The woman unceremoniously pulled her pants over the bandage and got dressed. "She was just sterilized!" Rinchen exclaimed after talking briefly with Dr. Tashi. I greeted Dr. Tashi and asked Rinchen to inquire how many children the woman had. "One child," she was told.

At the next table blood was pouring from a pregnant woman's vagina. Two doctors were trying to insert a rubber catheter into her urethra. Dr. Tashi explained for a long time in Tibetan before Rinchen translated, "There's some problem with this baby. The mother's got internal bleeding. The doctors feel the best thing to do is cut the whole thing out." At first I thought this meant they would perform a hysterectomy, but it turned out they were talking about a Caesarean section.

"Is this what they would do in the United States?" Rinchen asked. She was not reassured when I said yes. Dr. Tashi said that she had to work. I thanked her and asked if we could see the patients I had seen the other day. "*Mei wonti,*" she said—no problem.

"Isn't she cute," Rinchen said to a young mother and father holding their newborn daughter on the next bed. "It's their first baby," Rinchen told me. "They are in the performance business. He is in the Tibetan opera. She is a violin player. They are allowed to have a second child, but they have to wait three years. Otherwise, there is a 1,000-yuan fine."

Another patient's husband offered us large hunks of boiled lamb. "This man has five boys and six girls," Rinchen said. "Last year the Chinese implemented family planning in his village. They have eleven children. This will be their twelfth. According to the local officials, what is already born is born. Nothing to do. But this new one in the stomach is a problem. There is a fine but no one is sure how much it is. Apparently they are more strict with city folks, especially cadre workers. All of the other families in the room are passing comments like, 'He's going to take it out.' He is reluctant. He doesn't know what to do. He says he wants to have more children, especially if they're sons. His mentality is like counting his herd."

Lying under two blankets in the next bed, a woman told Rinchen that she was pregnant for the second time that year. She had lost the first baby. "She asked the doctors to please let her have this child but they insist that she have an abortion; the doctors say she will die if she has the child." Another woman at the end of the row said that the doctors were pressuring her to abort her second pregnancy. Both women felt well and wanted to deliver.

• • •

When we returned to the Barkhor, Rinchen's cousin was waiting outside her room at the Tibetan hotel. He had come by bus from Gyantse. When Rinchen saw him scratching, she started to pick nits from his head, throwing them over the wall. I went back to my hotel to retrieve a medicated shampoo that I was glad I had not needed to use. Rinchen was still nit-picking when I returned.

Under my direction Rinchen used warm water from my thermos to apply the shampoo to her cousin's head. While waiting ten minutes for the shampoo to work, I told her the lice would walk off by themselves if he stood on his head. Rinchen helped lift her cousin's feet above his head and held them against the wall. Neither he nor Rinchen questioned the *Inji amchi* (Western doctor), even after I said the lice would leave faster if he sang a song. Rinchen realized that I was playing a joke when her cousin started singing, but she did not say anything until he had finished. It was a rare moment of levity during my otherwise bleak return to Tibet.

* * *

There was no one around to translate when I saw Champa Tenzin for the last time to pick up the tape. In Tibetan we told each other that each of us, the Dalai Lama, and Tibet's freedom were all *yakbudoo*. Then we said farewell to each other. I carried Champa Tenzin's smile with me while I waited for my ride to the airport. I had documented more than I ever imagined would be possible; to stay any longer would only increase my chances of getting caught. I tried to assume the countenance of a happy tourist who would someday like to return to Tibet in order to spend more money.

I had enough video interviews to show that China was implementing a two-child family-planning policy for rural Tibetans, and a one-child policy for those in larger towns and cities. To enforce this a host of economic, social, and political sanctions had been established. Although some contraceptives were available, abortion and sterilization were the primary forms of birth control in Tibet. The implications of the mobile birth-control teams and eugenics programs in Amdo were particularly disturbing. I did not know if China was committing genocide in Tibet, but it was my belief that China's family-planning policy, and its colonization of Tibet, were having a genocidal effect on the Tibetans.

* * *

A Tibetan man gave me a ride to the airport at four in the morning in a dilapidated jeep that could only reach a top speed of thirty miles per hour. Tourist buses and Land Rovers passed us continually during the two hours it took to reach the airport. I arrived after the flight's scheduled departure, but found the mob of passengers still pushing to get through customs for our flight.

A soldier looked at my ticket and pointed to the date, which was for the previous day—I had inadvertently overstepped my two-day extension. "*Mei you*," she said. How well I'd come to know those words.

"Golden Dragon," I said. She smiled and stamped my ticket. She also ordered another soldier to carry my pack.

Soldiers walked back and forth along the line of passengers, who were kept standing outside the airplane for another half-hour in the frigid dawn air. I was the last person to get on the plane and the first to disembark in Chengdu. There, luckily, the customs agents were talking among themselves. I picked up my pack and casually walked past them. Looking back, I saw the agents beginning to search the long line of passengers.

I could not relax until I had cleared a second customs for a direct flight to Hong Kong. I wrote rock and roll titles on my video cassettes and befriended a Canadian couple who spoke Chinese and told me they loved China. They could tell that I was nervous and asked if something was wrong. I said that I had the *douza*.

Soldiers searched my pack thoroughly and found the video cassettes. One looked at the tapes carefully and asked what I had taken pictures of.

"Beautiful people," I said, as he leafed through my passport.

"Did you go to Tibet?"

"It was too cold," I said. The soldier waved me through.

EPILOGUE

....

BEFORE WITNESSING CHINA'S use of lethal force to suppress the nationalist demonstrations in Lhasa in the fall of 1987, I had no idea that I would spend much of the next six years investigating human rights violations in Tibet. Although this has often been a gruesome undertaking, I feel privileged to have met so many Tibetans I can characterize only as noble, and to have shared in their struggle for freedom.

On February 22, 1992, Champa Tenzin was found dead in his room in the Jokhang Temple. The police claimed it was a suicide. Tibetans in the Jokhang claimed he was murdered. One of Champa Tenzin's attendants found him in the morning with a rope tied around his neck, covered with blood. The other end of the rope was tied to the leg of the bed. Neither the bed nor the room were disturbed. The Lhasa PSB officials who examined the body declared it a suicide and made the head of the temple sign a document to that effect.

Under Chinese law, the case would be investigated, but none of Champa's relatives or the Jokhang monks were interviewed. When I learned all of this from a report by the Tibet Information Network in London, which never made it onto the international wire or into any papers in the United States, I immediately suspected that the Lhasa police had murdered Champa Tenzin. The most obvious sign of a police cover-up is the near impossibility of self-strangulation, which for that matter also would not lead to blood loss.

For me, Champa Tenzin's death epitomizes the Tibetan people's plight. Although China's brutal repression of independence demonstra-

tions throughout Tibet have awakened the world to Tibetan nationalism, the free world continues to prefer doing business with China rather
than hold China accountable for its atrocities in Tibet, and on the
mainland. If China's colonization of Tibet and enforced family-planning policies continue, the world will lose one of its most peaceful cultures. China and the West have much to learn from Tibet; but there is
little time left.

▪ Tingri, the staging point for all travelers approaching the Tibetan side of Mt. Everest.

▪ Cooking inside the tent of Tsarang, one of the yak men who helped lead us to Everest.

■ Looking up at the North Col on Everest from Camp III at 22,000 feet—the start of technical climbing.

■ The Potala, winter palace of the Dalai Lama.

■ The streets of Lhasa.

■ Overturned police vehicles burning during the October 1 protests in Lhasa.

■ Thousands of Tibetans filled the streets of Lhasa during the October 1 protests.

■ A twenty-five-year-old Tibetan man shot through the heart by Chinese police during protests.

■ A man carrying his ten-year-old son after the boy was shot in the chest during the protests.

■ Two monks running into the burning police station to rescue others trapped inside during October 1 protests.

■ Tibetans escaping from the side of the burning police station.

■ Champa Tenzin, a monk whose dramatic escape from the burning police station inspired the protesting crowds.

■ John Ackerly (right) and myself with the Dali Lama in Dharamsala, northern India, seat of the Tibetan government-in-exile.

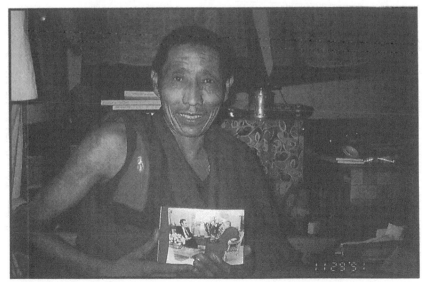

■ Champa Tenzin in the Jokhang Temple in 1991, holding his prized photo of the Dali Lama meeting with George Bush.